Culturally Sustaining Language and Literacy Practices for Pre-K–3 Classrooms

The Children Come Full

Kindel Turner Nash, Alicia Arce-Boardman,
Roderick D. Peele, and Kerry Elson

Foreword by Gloria S. Boutte

Teachers College Press
TEACHERS COLLEGE | COLUMBIA UNIVERSITY
NEW YORK AND LONDON

Published by Teachers College Press,® 1234 Amsterdam Avenue, New York, NY 10027

Copyright © 2022 by Teachers College, Columbia University

Front cover illustration by Erik J. Sumner (www.BrownCrayon.com). Front cover design by Edwin Kuo.

All rights reserved. No part of this publication may be reproduced or transmitted in any form or by any means, electronic or mechanical, including photocopy, or any information storage and retrieval system, without permission from the publisher. For reprint permission and other subsidiary rights requests, please contact Teachers College Press, Rights Dept.: tcpressrights@tc.columbia.edu

Library of Congress Cataloging-in-Publication Data is available at loc.gov

ISBN 978-0-8077-6746-7 (paper)
ISBN 978-0-8077-6747-4 (hardcover)
ISBN 978-0-8077-8128-9 (ebook)

Printed on acid-free paper
Manufactured in the United States of America

THE CULTURALLY SUSTAINING PEDAGOGIES SERIES

SERIES EDITOR: Django Paris, *University of Washington*

ADVISORY BOARD: H. Samy Alim, Maggie Beneke, Jeremy Garcia, Gloria Ladson-Billings, Tiffany Lee, Danny Martinez, Teresa McCarty, Timothy San Pedro, Valerie Shirley

The overarching purpose of the Culturally Sustaining Pedagogies (CSP) Series is to offer preparing and practicing educators, graduate students, and scholars a comprehensive series of books dedicated to educational settings engaged in sustaining Indigenous, Black, Latinx, Asian, and Pacific Islander young people, families, and communities as these memberships necessarily intersect with gender and sexuality, disability, migration, language, land, class, and more. The CSP Series is defined by its coherent focus on the strengths and wisdom of young people, families, elders, communities, and educators who use education—in Pre-K through college classrooms, across content areas, in community organizations, and in peer and family settings—as a tool of positive social transformation and revitalization.

Culturally Sustaining Language and Literacy Practices for Pre-K–3 Classrooms:
The Children Come Full
KINDEL TURNER NASH, ALICIA ARCE-BOARDMAN,
RODERICK D. PEELE, AND KERRY ELSON

Native Presence and Sovereignty in College:
Sustaining Indigenous Weapons to Defeat Systemic Monsters
AMANDA R. TACHINE

Culturally Relevant Pedagogy:
Asking a Different Question
GLORIA LADSON-BILLINGS

Protecting the Promise:
Indigenous Education Between Mothers and Their Children
TIMOTHY SAN PEDRO

Toni Morrison wrote, "If there is a book you want to read, but it hasn't been written yet, then you must write it." To the children of Northern Parkway and Central Park East 2, who, as Haydée Dohrn-Melendez Morgan says, "Come as full humans, full people, full," and to early childhood preservice teachers everywhere. We wrote this book for you.

Contents

Series Foreword *Django Paris*		xi
Foreword *Gloria S. Boutte*		xiii
Preface		xv
Acknowledgments		xvii

1. **The Children Come Full: Toward a Framework for Culturally Sustaining Early Literacy Teaching** — 1
   Kindel Turner Nash, Alicia Arce-Boardman, Roderick Peele, Kerry Elson, and Haydée Dohrn-Melendez Morgan

We Wrote This Book for You	2
Guiding Definitions	3
Theory as a North Star	3
Culturally Sustaining Early Literacy Teaching	6
Culturally Sustaining Early Literacy Teaching: An Interpretive Framework	9
Book Authors and School Contexts	9
An Invitation	12

2. **No Behavior Charts: Building Sustaining Learning Communities for Young Children** — 13
   Kindel Turner Nash, Alicia Arce-Boardman, Roderick Peele, Kerry Elson, and Haydée Dohrn-Melendez Morgan

Before the School Year Begins	14
Setting Up the Classroom	18
Norms, Routines, Conflicts, and Celebrations	24
Conclusion	33

3. **Sustaining Beginnings: Literacy Practices to Foster Knowing and Being Known**   34
   Kindel Turner Nash, Alicia Arce-Boardman, Roderick Peele, and Kerry Elson

   Fostering Knowingness Through Morning Meetings   35

   Share Time   37

   Knowingness Through Naming: Labeling the Classroom   37

   Knowingness Through the Classroom Library   39

   Child-Created Book-Basket Labels   39

   Knowingness Through Creating Identity Texts   40

   Creating Critical Spaces Through Read-Alouds   43

   Knowingness Through Letter, Sound, and Word Work   45

   Beginning the Reading and Writing Workshop   48

   Conclusion   52

4. **"¿Que Piensas?"/"What Do You Think?": Culturally Sustaining Ways of Reading**   53
   Kindel Turner Nash, Alicia Arce-Boardman, Roderick Peele, and Kerry Elson

   How Do Children Learn to Read?   54

   Culturally Sustaining Reading Practices   61

   Life-Affirming Ways of Reading   61

   Classroom Library   61

   Conclusion   70

5. **I Am Enough: Culturally Sustaining Approaches to Oral Language and Vocabulary Development**   71
   Kindel Turner Nash, Alicia Arce-Boardman, Roderick Peele, and Kerry Elson

   All Children Have Impressive Language Abilities   72

   Oral Language Development   72

   Fostering Oral Language Development Through Talk and Play   73

   Vocabulary Development   80

   Conclusion: I Am Enough   87

6.	**"Just Because My Parents Are From El Salvador You Can't Say They Are Bad and Evil": Culturally Sustaining Ways of Writing**	**89**
	Kindel Turner Nash, Alicia Arce-Boardman, Roderick Peele, and Kerry Elson	
	How Do Children Learn to Write?	90
	Culturally Sustaining Writing Instruction	97
	Conclusion	109
7.	**Attending to Children: Literacy Assessment That Cultivates Joy and Genius**	**111**
	Kindel Turner Nash, Alicia Arce-Boardman, Roderick Peele, and Kerry Elson	
	A Word About Standardized and High-Stakes Assessments	112
	Vocabulary	121
	Spelling and Phonemic Awareness	122
	Conclusion	124
8.	**An Epilogue: The Truth That's Already There**	**125**
	Kindel Turner Nash, Alicia Arce-Boardman, Roderick Peele, and Kerry Elson with Haydée Dohrn-Melendez Morgan	
	Missteps and Tensions	128
	The Children Come Full	129

Appendix A: Children's Literature for Creating and Sustaining Communities	**131**
References	**134**
Index	**149**
About the Authors	**155**

Series Foreword

Greetings! I am so glad you have opened this wonderful book. I am particularly happy if you are a person dedicated to centering and sustaining the youngest learners in our communities and classrooms. Indeed, as Kindel Turner Nash, Alicia Arce-Boardman, Roderick D. Peele, and Kerry Elson write early in the book, "We wrote this book for you, because we know you believe in the promise of Indigenous, Black, Latinx, and Asian and Pacific Islander and other marginalized children, families, and communities" (p. 2). The authors, a teacher-educator and advocate and a brilliant group of early childhood teachers, carry this invitation across the pages of the book.

Also in the early pages, the authors share the words of Haydée Dohrn-Melendez Morgan, one of the culturally sustaining educators we are gifted to learn with in this book: "Children come full, they come as full humans, full people, full." It is the truth of these words that the teachers and children at the heart of this book seek to share and amplify, that young children come full and it is our work as educators to join them in that fullness. As H. Samy Alim and I have written, culturally sustaining pedagogy (CSP) sees the outcome of learning as additive rather than subtractive, as remaining whole rather than being framed as broken, as critically enriching strengths rather than replacing deficits. It is this wholeness, this fullness, that this book invites us to join through language and literacy teaching and learning.

One of the striking things about this book is that it takes your hand and leads you through classrooms, through days, weeks, and moments—a lesson, an interaction. It helps you see and envision multiple ways of setting up a classroom, joining young children in daily routines, and reading and writing with them in loving and sustaining ways. This is to say it is a profoundly concrete and theoretically grounded set of practices and processes we are gifted with by the fullness of these young people and their teachers. But we are led not in a way that is prescriptive, for CSP is not a prescriptive theory of teaching. Rather, this book takes our hand and leads us into learning in a way that invites and inspires and leads us toward taking these gifts into our own practice, our own dreaming.

In Gloria Boutte's foreword that follows my words here, she writes, "The authors . . . show us in example after example ways in which educators can sustain communal love" (p. xiii). Boutte's meditation on sustaining communal love is so important. It leads me to recognize that what we really witness in this book are portraits of loved teachers loving young children in their fullness. As the authors share:

> [These teachers] are exemplary because love notes from budding pre-K writers fill up whole walls in Haydée's classroom. Because children say "the best thing about last year was my teacher, Kerry." Because they bring Alicia her favorite coffee drink the day after giving her a rough time and eagerly share stories from home during every morning meeting. Because Roderick's class was so engaged that 90% were able to log in to online school on that first pandemic day—full of questions about life and school. They are loved because they strive to understand how children develop and grow as full humans and as readers, speakers, and writers. (p. 3)

This comment about Rodrick's class on that first day of pandemic teaching deserves further attention. I do not know where we will be as a society and as a world when you pick up this book. I do know that the confluence of pandemic, climate crisis, and emboldened white supremacy, as well as the beautiful ongoing movements for decolonization and intersectional justice, will continue to influence how we teach, learn, and live and how we resist, remember, and reimagine. And I know, as the teachers, children, and families in this book show us time and time again, that Black, Indigenous, Latinx, Asian, Pacific Islander and all global majority young people and their communities will continue to come full. Educators committed to centering and sustaining that fullness across the early years and far beyond will welcome this book into their learning. Many thanks to Kindel, Alicia, Roderick, Kerry, and Haydée for opening their classrooms doors—and their hearts—so that we may teach and learn alongside them.

—Django Paris,
University of Washington on Coast Salish Lands

Foreword

When Jonathan, my son, was born in 1996, one of my favorite books to read to him was *So Much* by Trish Cooke (1994). I was drawn to the book because it served as a mirror for our family life. As the family in the book gathers for a birthday celebration for the father of an African American baby boy, extended family members, including a grandmother, aunt, uncle, and cousins, enter at staggered times. Everyone who comes in the house focuses on the baby boy first before engaging in communal activities like dancing, play-fighting, playing dominoes, playing cards, and simply enjoying each other's company. The love that Black families have for children is illuminated in this book. Also satisfying to me is the author's use of African American Language (AAL) to tell the story. She uses a version of AAL often heard in New Orleans, the place from which my children's paternal family hails. In this AAL style, adjectives are sometimes repeated three times for emphasis. For instance, in the story, the refrain says, "And the house was full, full, full." For me, this conveyed a deep level of satisfaction, joy, and completion. There is a lot going on simultaneously, and all of it feels *full* and just right.

Culturally Sustaining Language and Literacy Practices for Pre-K–3 Classrooms: The Children Come Full invites educators to recognize this *fullness* that Children and Families of Color bring into our educational spaces. Posing the larger question, *In what ways is culture central to literacy learning?*, the authors illustrate effective and engaging literacy practices that build on the wisdom and beauty that Children of Color bring to school. This book offers strategies for teachers to create homes-away-from-homes for children. The authors, a teacher-educator and three early childhood teachers, show us in example after example ways in which educators can sustain communal love.

And speaking of love—revolutionary love, which at once affirms children and their families and seeks to dismantle oppression, Kindel, Alicia, Haydée, Roderick, and Kerry skillfully demonstrate what fullness looks and feels like through the experiences of three teachers. Theory meets practice as the authors paint portraits of classroom spaces where teachers, children, and students learn and thrive—and are happy to be there. As writer Zora Neale Hurston once said, "Love makes your soul crawl out from its hiding place." In these classrooms, young children can be themselves and authentic literacies flourish. Children are allowed to bring their whole selves into the classroom.

The teachers' commitment, enthusiasm, and love come through loud and clear in each chapter. Reflecting on preparing the environment for the children before school begins, they suggest that classrooms should be simple and bare. This leaves room for the imprints from all of the *full* children and their ideas. This is so much better than the prepackaged, heavily teacher-influenced setup that we all have provided at one time or another. What a refreshing idea! If classrooms are truly going to be loving community spaces, children's influence should be apparent. Ideas for facilitating cultural continuity between schools and homes are abundant.

This book provides ideas for new and experienced teachers alike. Teachers who are trying to figure out ways to center children's home languages while also teaching reading, writing, and developing orality will find robust recommendations in this text. Music and play are central to these early childhood spaces. Readers will finish the book, which will no doubt be used as an ongoing resource, and think, "Children and teachers *want* to be in educational spaces like this." Indeed, the examples shared will help create early childhood literacy spaces that are *full, full, full* of love—just like the children.

—Gloria S. Boutte

Preface

This book shares culturally sustaining early literacy teaching grounded in three teacher-coauthors' practices and processes. We will offer definitions of literacy, culture, and principles of culturally sustaining early literacy pedagogies, as well as a model and interpretive framework for culturally sustaining early literacy teaching that can be applied to six facets of early language and literacy: (1) learning in/with children and communities, (2) literacy routines and procedural knowledge, (3) teaching reading, (4) developing oral language and vocabulary, (5) teaching writing, and (6) literacy assessment. Through connecting and contextualizing these facets with the goals and features of culturally sustaining pedagogies, educators can work toward hybridizing and transforming their practices to *sustain* Indigenous, Black, Latinx, Asian and Pacific Islander children, families, and communities.

HOW TO USE THIS BOOK

This book is written with an audience of early childhood preservice teachers in mind, although inservice teachers, administrators, professional developers, literacy coaches, graduate students, and researchers may find it useful. We envision this volume being used as a core text in early/elementary literacy teaching and assessment courses. Through vivid examples, the book addresses a range of pressing topics based on an extensive examination of literature on language and literacy, and culture and the burgeoning literature on culturally sustaining pedagogies (CSPs).

To make the book clear and accessible, each chapter includes focus questions, an opening story, visuals, illustrative tables, and artifacts. Literature, examples, and learning experiences are interwoven throughout Chapters 2–7 to guide readers' thinking and implementation in their own contexts. A conclusion at the end of each chapter provides a brief review of the chapter. The references and book index may also be of interest, in addition to the authors' personal website associated with this book, childrencomefull.com. Chapter 8 synthesizes key ideas and a vision for moving toward culturally sustaining early literacy teaching. Appendix A contains a list of children's literature highlighted throughout the book.

Acknowledgments

First, I overwhelmingly acknowledge my elders, Lloyce Nelson, Earl Turner, and Allison Tillinghast; you model wisdom, excellence, and grace through the way you love and live. Endless appreciation goes to Drs. Gloria Boutte, Etta Ruth Hollins, and Susi Long; your guidance and mentorship make me a better person. I am ever grateful to Otha Malik Nash for your love and ruminations. And I extend many thanks to Anisa, Taj, Salim, and Karim Nash; you challenge and inspire me every day. I owe gratitude to Bilal Polson, principal and brother extraordinaire. To my sister scholars Joy Howard, Candace Thompson, Timberly Baker, Keisha McIntosh Allen, Kyla Thomas, Sakeena Everett, Amy Swain, Katya Strekalova-Hughes, Leah Panther, Sophia Rodriguez and my sisters Sarah Tillinghast, Mary Stevens, Elena Hampton-Stover, and Elena Illardi—you nurture me in only the ways sister scholars and sisters can.

—Kindel Turner Nash

Kindel, it has been an amazing opportunity to be able to share this space with you. Thank you for trusting me and helping me grow as an educator and writer. Dr. Bilal Polson, thank you for introducing me to the National Council of Teachers of English (NCTE) Professional Dyads in Culturally Relevant Teaching (PDCRT) and for the space you have created within the Northern Parkway School for me to grow. I am forever thankful for my friendship with Jessica Martell, who continues to inspire me and my instructional practices. Thank you to my husband, Jeff, for always building me up and never allowing me to stop. Thank you to my children, Kayla, Jenna, and Chase, for being my number one inspiration. I am forever grateful to my parents, Edward and Nelly Arce, for their love and guidance. Finally, I thank my sisters, Debora and Michelle, for their unending love and support.

—Alicia Arce-Boardman

I acknowledge Alicia for recognizing the contributions I could offer to this work. To Shamika Simpson, thank you for inspiring me to go forth into the world of education. Dr. Monique Habersham, thank you for being the first to see what was inside of me as an educator. I am grateful to Dr. Bilal Polson, Principal of Northern Parkway School. Thanks to my ancestors who worked tirelessly laying the foundation for this work. To my wife: you inspire me through your intellect and dedication to your personal pursuits; thank you for your willingness to support me, my scholars, and their families. Appreciation goes out to my family for your love and support. Lastly, to my late grandparents, Jonah Peele, Sr., and Katherine Rodgers-Peele. You have had the greatest impact on me; there are no words I could ever put together to express my love, appreciation, and gratitude for you both.

—Roderick Peele

Many thanks to Kindel, for inviting me to contribute to this book and for being an invaluable inspiration and thought partner; to Naomi Smith, principal of Central Park East (CPE) 2, and Theresa Luongo, assistant principal of CPE 2, for hiring me and trusting me; to my friend Thomas Vorsteg for being my sounding board and finding the joy and humor in everything; to Pamela Jones, for her guidance and for helping me become a better teacher; and to my parents, Marjorie and Tony Elson, and my sister, Amanda Elson, for their endless support!

—Kerry Elson

CHAPTER 1

The Children Come Full
Toward a Framework for Culturally Sustaining Early Literacy Teaching

*Kindel Turner Nash, Alicia Arce-Boardman, Roderick Peele,
Kerry Elson, and Haydée Dohrn-Melendez Morgan*

> Children come full, they come as full humans, full people, full. They come full with many different experiences . . . and [we] get to be present in this kind of beautiful, uninhibited way of understanding that feels so, that *is* so brilliant. Our world does a good job of trying to erase some of that, who they are, of not being allowed to claim it, so it's our job not to let that happen.
>
> —Haydée Dohrn-Melendez Morgan

Haydée's words expressed her belief in the *fullness* of children; her ideas resonate with all of us and embody the story we hope to tell in this book. We believe in the fullness of children and in creating classrooms that sustain that fullness. For over a decade, Kindel has spent time with high-performing literacy teachers in urban schools across the United States in order to understand their highly effective and culturally sustaining practices. Children in urban schools are often faced with scripted curricula and standardized instructional practices requiring minimal critical thinking (Adair, 2014; Anyon, 1980; Delpit, 2006; Domínguez, 2017). There, children internalize the idea that school is merely a place for them to comply and complete rote tasks (Adair, 2014; Beneke, 2019). We know all of this. Yet, while there is much talk about what is *not working* in urban schools—guided by elders Etta Hollins, Gloria Boutte, and Susi Long—Kindel sought to understand what was *already working* (Ladson-Billings, 2017). Informed by humanizing research methods

---

Focus Questions: In what ways is culture central to literacy learning? How have approaches to literacy instruction changed over time? How can you interpret literacy practices for specific contexts?

(Paris & Winn, 2013; San Pedro & Kinloch, 2017), Kindel observed and documented the literacy practices of a total of 60 teachers; this book focuses on four Pre-K–3rd-grade teachers, Haydée Dohrn-Melendez Morgan (Chapters 1–2) and Alicia Arce-Boardman, Roderick Peele, and Kerry Elson (Chapters 1–8). Camangian and Cariaga (2021) ask teachers to consider whether our practices are colonizing or *life-affirming*. This book offers a multifaceted model and culturally sustaining, humanizing, and life-affirming practices that we feel honor and extend the *fullness* of children.

WE WROTE THIS BOOK FOR YOU

We wrote this book for you, because we know you believe in the promise of Indigenous, Black, Latinx, and Asian and Pacific Islander and other marginalized children, families, and communities. You believe in the fullness of children and families and want to honor and sustain it through your teaching. Yet, solutions offered and marketed as a solution to the problem of low literacy proficiency have focused on children's and families' perceived *deficits* rather than on their *strengths* (Doucet & Adair, 2018; Paris & Alim, 2014). Deficit perspectives "view the languages, literacies, and cultural ways of being of many students and communities of color as deficiencies to be overcome" (Paris & Alim, 2014, p. 87) and focus on "how to get working-class students of color to speak and write more like middle-class White[s]" (Paris & Alim, 2014, p. 87). They advance damage-centered narratives (Tuck, 2009) that suggest that children need to develop grit, change their maladaptive social and emotional behaviors, fill gaps in their word knowledge they lack from home, or rise up out of a culture of poverty. Deficit solutions and discourses center on a panoptic White gaze and divide urban schools and communities (Morrison, 1998). We write against these solutions, for you.

More than a century of research suggests that literacy teaching should center on children's family, history, culture, and language (Au, 1979; Boutte, 2015; Cooper, 1892; Gay, 2017; Genishi & Dyson, 2009; Hollins, 2015a; Muhammad, 2020; Nash et al., 2020; Paris & Alim, 2017a; Woodson, 1933). Yet early literacy research has emphasized linear, acultural approaches (Hoffman et al., 2021; Stahl & Yaden, 2004). Linear models view learning as a hierarchical process—a line of regression (Nash & Piña, 2020). As a result, within these predominant models, learning to read is framed as a simple formula (Hollins, 2017; Street & Street, 1984; Yatvin, 2002). This has resulted in standardized, ready-made literacy practices touted as effective for all contexts. Viewing learning as a line of regression demands that children get "ready" to master a defined set of skills (Yoon, 2015). We write against that research, for you.

Alicia, Roderick, Kerry, and Haydée are exemplary literacy teachers. We know that not just because they have won awards (they have) or because each year their students experience academic and social growth (they do). They are exemplary because love notes from budding pre-K writers fill up whole walls in Haydée's classroom. Because children say "the best thing about last year was my teacher, Kerry." Because they bring Alicia her favorite coffee drink the day after giving her a rough time and eagerly share stories from home during every morning meeting. Because Roderick's class was so engaged that 90% were able to log in to online school on that first pandemic day—full of questions about life and school. They are loved because they strive to understand how children develop and grow as full humans and as readers, speakers, and writers. They know how to help children who seem to struggle—and if they don't, they try to figure it out. They know the children in their classes and their families and communities well. If you are looking to nurture these capacities within your own teacher-self, we wrote this book for you.

GUIDING DEFINITIONS

In this book, we take up the following definitions of *literacy, culture,* and *culturally sustaining literacy teaching practices.* These definitions frame the way we think and talk about practices and counterpractices throughout the book.

> *Literacy* is the ability to read, write, listen, visualize, and talk about multiple kinds of texts. The way people read, write, listen, visualize, and talk is socially, culturally, linguistically, and historically situated within disciplines, contexts, structural inequities, and systems of oppression (Frankel et al., 2016; Larson & Marsh, 2015).
> *Culture* is our complex psychological, sociological, and spiritual makeup and how we integrate ancestral knowledge as it exists in our cultures, languages, and communities' patterns of knowing, being, and doing in the world (Hollins, 2015a).
> *Culturally sustaining literacy teaching practices* are purposefully sequenced, interconnected, iterative progressions of experiences that mediate, extend, and sustain children's local, indigenous, culturally situated ancestral knowledge to support cumulative and increasingly complex understandings of language and literacy (Nash & Panther, 2019).

THEORY AS A NORTH STAR

The guiding definitions are deeply rooted in our theories about learning. Love (2019) calls educational theory her "North Star . . . a steadfast tool to explain without fluff or gimmicks . . . our students' realities" (p. 132). Our North Star theories are humanizing and liberatory. They help us understand the centrality of culture and the importance of learning in and with communities, which we believe are necessary to enact culturally sustaining literacy teaching.

Specifically, we draw from the overlapping perspectives of social-constructivist, humanizing, sociocultural, and critical sociocultural educational theories. These theories foster our understanding of early literacy practices and policies that can create sites of possibility for equitable participation in a pluralistic society. Our North Star theories guide our beliefs about what children and communities know and can do. Culturally sustaining pedagogies compose a "critical, anti-racist, anti-colonial framework that rejects the white settler capitalist gaze and the kindred cisheteropatriarchal, English-monolingual, ableist, classist, xenophobic, and other hegemonic gazes" (Paris, 2021, p. 261). We need theoretical perspectives that guide us toward humanization, criticality, and ultimately liberation (see Figure 1.1).

Humanizing, liberatory theories that foster cultural sustenance have always existed to help people envision an *elsewhere* beyond society and its standardized and colonizing institutions and to imagine an *otherwise* world, a space beyond the present systems of domination and oppression (Dumas, 2014; Grande & McCarty, 2018). For example, Muhammad (2020) notes that throughout the 1800s, a central goal among Black people in the United States was to improve and elevate their lives through literacy. In contrast to theories that serve to colonize, standardize, or offer decontextualized reforms, critical sociocultural, humanizing, and culturally sustaining theories advance the importance of human connection (del Carmen Salazar, 2013).

Put another way, critical sociocultural, humanizing, culturally sustaining perspectives hold that children "are not uniform; the nature and extent of their literacy experiences are shaped by cultural, linguistic, and socioeconomic factors, along with personal interests and situational dynamics" (Dyson, 2013, p. 5). Arguing that context determines content (Glossop, 1988) within these approaches, teachers "take into account aspects of youths' lives outside

Figure 1.1. North Star Learning Theories

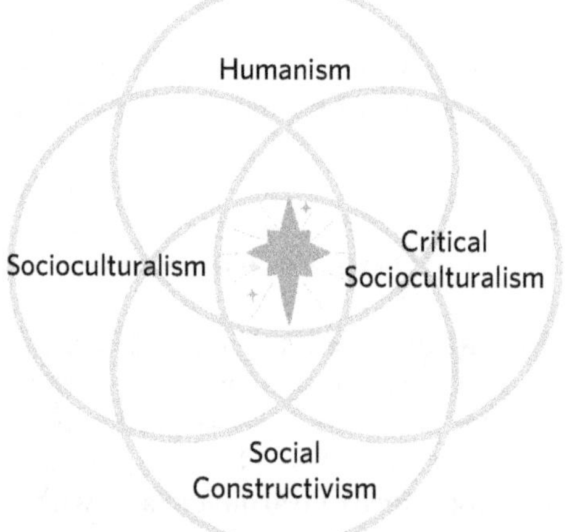

the classroom not only as resources, but as targets of learning to be sustained" (Lee, 2017, p. 262). Critical sociocultural, humanizing, and culturally sustaining theories come together to form our North Star. Table 1.1 provides a detailed description of each of these theoretical perspectives.

Table 1.1. Learning Theories, Traits, and Practices

Theory	Traits	Practices
Humanism	Learning to be literate is a vehicle for overcoming personal hardship and fulfilling human potential.	• Ensuring that children's basic needs are met • Building strong relationships with children and families • Culturally authentic classroom library, reading texts based on student's funds of knowledge • Language revitalization through teaching students' heritage languages • Afrocentric teaching to confront anti-Blackness
Critical Socioculturalism	Learning and teaching literacy within a historicized, sociocultural, sociopolitical context, and actively attending to children's and community's identity, power, privilege, oppression, and justice.	• Building deep relationships with families and communities • Evaluating the classroom library, or responding in writing to current sociopolitical events • Translanguaging • Creating identity texts • Creating multimodal texts • Decolonizing approaches to language revitalization through teaching students' heritage languages • Hybridized reading and writing workshop • Interactive read-aloud of authentic texts
Socioculturalism	Learning and teaching literacy in a way that frames and mediates culture within relational and dialogic zones of proximal development.	• Using children's language and other cultural referents in classroom texts (e.g., messages) • Getting to know families and communities • Reading and writing workshop using a gradual release of responsibility approach • Reading aloud texts that build on students' funds of knowledge • Conferring with students

(continued)

Table 1.1. *(continued)*

Theory	Traits	Practices
Social Constructivism	Learning to read involves each person in unique thinking processes, interaction, and responses to meaningful, functional, authentic literature and text.	• Reading purposefully integrated into content area instruction based on children's interests • Modeling reading and writing through interactive reading and writing experiences • Strategy instruction • Gradual release of responsibility • Reading and writing workshop • Project-based learning

CULTURALLY SUSTAINING EARLY LITERACY TEACHING

In the book *Toward Culturally Sustaining Teaching: Early Childhood Educators Honor Children with Practices for Equity and Change* (Nash et al., 2020), the authors describe culturally sustaining pedagogies (CSPs) using the metaphor of a family tree. The family tree visualizes culturally rooted and asset-based early literacy teaching practices as being linked to a rich lineage of sociopolitical and legal actions and as having a multifaceted root system of liberation scholarship by Black, Latinx, Indigenous, and Pacific Islander people. Ladson-Billings (2014) and Paris (2012) have described CSPs as a recent, important outgrowth of culturally rooted, asset-based pedagogies, and culturally relevant teaching (Ladson-Billings, 1995, 2009). Culturally relevant teaching focuses on three key areas, developing students'

1. competence in their own and at least one other culture,
2. critical consciousness to fight against injustices, and
3. academic achievement (Ladson-Billings, 1995, 2009).

We believe that both culturally relevant and culturally sustaining teaching are crucial. As 2nd-grade teacher Janice Baines reminds us, "if we do not see relevance in the lives and histories that are most marginalized . . . we will not have the foundation needed to liberate, emancipate, or sustain relevance" (Baines et al., 2018, p. 12). However, striving to move beyond relevance or responsiveness to students' cultural assets, CSPs are the fruits of that family tree. CSPs embrace a vision of racial justice and liberation divested from the specter of racial violence and colonial logic that often tries to cloud that vision (Paris, 2021; see Figure 1.2). As such, Alim et al. (2020) have defined CSPs as "a critical framework for centering and sustaining Indigenous, Black, Latinx, Asian and Pacific Islander communities as these memberships necessarily intersect with gender and sexuality, disability, class, language, land, and more."

Cautioning against static, one-directional views of culture, in a 2017b interview with *Education Week*, Paris and Alim identified five features of CSPs

Figure 1.2. A Family Tree of Culturally Rooted Pedagogies

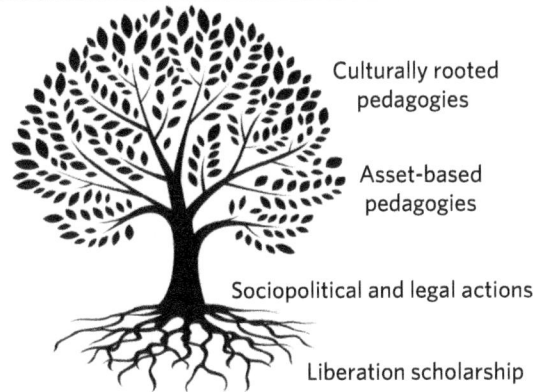

in practice. As the body of research and practice around CSPs has continued to evolve and grow, collectively, CSP scholar-activists have enhanced and identified further iterations (Eagle-Shield et al., 2020; Paris, 2021). Applied to the language and literacy teaching of young children, these collective features include the following:

1. Critically centering children's literacies, languages, and knowledge
2. Valuing children's and communities' agency and input so that we are accountable to the communities we serve
3. Historicizing content and instruction to connect learning to the histories of racial, ethnic, and linguistic communities, neighborhoods and cities, and the larger states and nation-states
4. Building children's and our own capacity to contend with internalized oppressions and to counter messages and systems that suggest that marginalized students and families are the problem and that value White, middle-class, monolingual, monocultural norms
5. Working with children and communities to sustain right, reciprocal relationships with the land
6. Curricularizing these features in learning settings

CSPs are critical to teaching that is liberatory and humanizing. In literature about CSPs in early childhood, Boutte and Muller (2018), Machado (2017), Doucet (2017), Osorio (2020), Laman and Henderson (2018), Wynter-Hoyte et al., (2019), Beneke (2019), and others highlight culturally sustaining *counterpractices*. *Counterpractices* are practices that depart from or counter official, standardized, or sanctioned practices. Counterpractices, many of which you will read about in this book, include creating identity texts, code-meshing, critical read-alouds, translanguaging, and more. Critical sociocultural and humanizing theories underpin counterpractices, recognizing that "education of any kind is inherently political and embedded within power structures that dictate privilege as well as bias and oppression" (Long et al., 2013, p. 422).

Building on the above features of CSPs and current literature on CSPs in early childhood, we strive to shine a light on CSPs in early literacy contexts. Based on our extensive investigation of culturally sustaining early literacy teaching in the teachers' classrooms, we have developed a model of culturally sustaining early literacy teaching. In this model, culturally sustaining early literacy teaching is viewed as being embedded within school and classroom communities of practice. As such, it is initiated by *processes* that are constantly in motion along the fluid dimensions of culturally sustaining, humanizing *practices* (see Figure 1.3). These processes and practices mediate the multiple layers of a child's lived experiences, or their ecosystem. Ecosystems structure a child's goals, engagement in and outside of school, tools for construction and representation, and ideas of what is possible over time (Dyson, 2013; Lee, 2017). Rather than a line of regression, which is often used to describe children's literacy learning through discrete stages, this model represents active and reciprocal learning rooted in knowledge of the literacy learning processes and children's and communities' ways of knowing, being, and reading. In this way, culturally sustaining early literacy learning processes can be visualized as a hyperbolic plane—an organic figure with many simultaneous inputs and outputs (Nash & Piña, 2020) (see Figure 1.3).

Figure 1.3. Culturally Sustaining Early Literacy Teaching Model

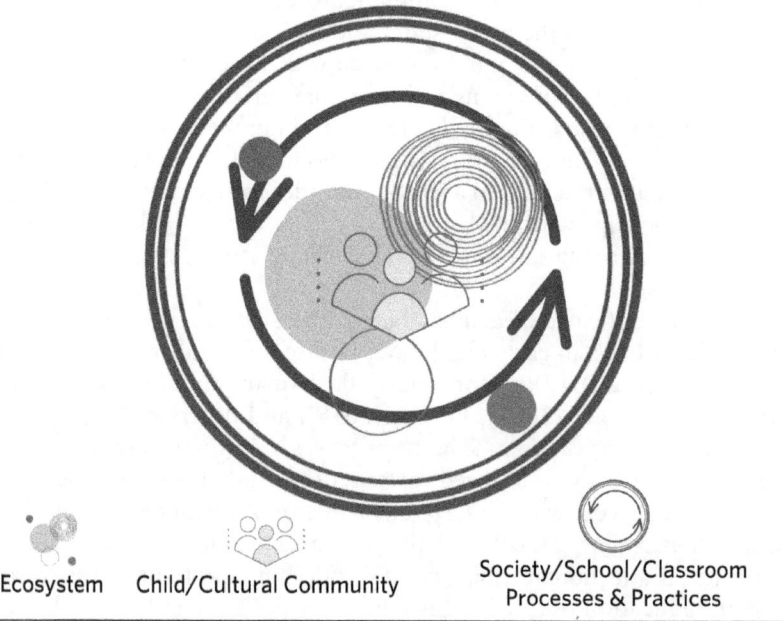

CULTURALLY SUSTAINING EARLY LITERACY TEACHING: AN INTERPRETIVE FRAMEWORK

Consistent with the model of culturally sustaining early literacy teaching (see Figure 1.3), an interpretive framework (see Figure 1.4) can be used as a tool to understand the literacy practices you will read about in this book. This interpretive framework builds on Hollins' (2011, 2015b) conception of *learning teaching as an interpretive process* (LTIP). LTIP positions teaching as an iterative process involving ongoing student-centered analysis through teaching and learning cycles. A learning cycle is a progression of experiences through which a child internalizes understandings of concepts, skills, strategies, processes, and phenomena. Teaching cycles apply knowledge of literacy to planning, enacting, interpreting, translating, revising, and reenacting instruction (Hollins, 2019). Moving away from the replication of core practices of expert teachers, LTIP insists on *teaching from the center* (Hollins, 2019). In other words, "the focus is not on the teacher's ability to represent, decompose, and approximate core practices, but on . . . interpreting and adapting practices to be highly effective in local, discipline-specific ways, always focusing on learner[s]" (Nash & Panther, 2019). This means "using essential knowledge about students, their everyday experiences and observations in the home and community and their cultural and ancestral knowledge in framing the curriculum and designing learning experiences" (Hollins, 2019, p. 38).

We conceptualize locations, actions, and impacts of teaching grounded in culturally sustaining and humanizing principles. Learning needs to be *situated, mediated, filtered,* and *implemented* within ecological, instructional, curricular contexts. This means that teachers must engage in a daily practice of self-reflection about children's and communities' needs as these needs are connected to technical literacy knowledge. The impact of interpretive teaching is community accountability and agency, contending with oppression, and critically centering children, families, and Communities of Color.

BOOK AUTHORS AND SCHOOL CONTEXTS

Alicia Arce-Boardman is currently in her 14th year teaching as a bilingual and dual-language education teacher in a public elementary school. She currently teaches 2nd and 3rd grade dual language in a loop, meaning that she teaches the same students for 2 school years. Alicia identifies as Latinx—her mother's family is from Paraguay and her father's is from Mexico. Alicia's explicit dedication to culturally relevant teaching began in 2013, when she was a participant in the Professional Dyads and Culturally Relevant Teaching (PDCRT) project through the National Council of Teachers of English, which pairs a classroom teacher with a university professor to explore culturally relevant teaching. Alicia strives to foreground children's voices as she works as a guide in the classroom community. This thinking drives her as not only an

Figure 1.4. An Interpretive Framework for Culturally Sustaining Early Childhood Pedagogies

Academic Knowledge	Cultural Knowledge	Critical Consciousness
Learning Contexts	**Epistemic Practices**	**Culturally Sustaining Pedagogies**
Ecological and cultural context(s)	Learning in, with, and about communities	Engaging student/community agency, input, and accountability
School's instructional and curricular practices	Technical and pedagogical knowledge of literacy	Historicizing curriculum and content
Teacher's philosophical stance and theoretical framework: "North Star"	Self-knowledge, societal knowledge, and understanding of learning theory	Contending with their own and children's internalized oppression
Cycles of teaching based on a child's needs	Understanding the cultural nature of human development	Critically centering children and communities

Interpretation → Translation → Liberation

educator but also as a wife and mother. When Alicia is not teaching children and college students, she enjoys being a dance mom and traveling with her husband and three children.

Roderick Peele is currently in his 8th year of teaching in two different public school districts. Roderick has taught 1st-, 2nd-, 3rd-, and 5th-grade scholars from inclusion to general settings. Currently, he teaches 2nd and 3rd grade in a loop. Roderick identifies as Black and is a descendant of African ancestors who were enslaved in the southern region of the United States. Roderick's encounters with culturally relevant teaching took place during his 2nd year of teaching, when he searched for more books with Black and Latinx protagonists and stumbled across Dr. Gloria Ladson-Billings's work. Even though she coined the title, at age 13 Roderick had already been introduced to these ideas within the book *The Mis-Education of the Negro* by Dr. Carter G. Woodson. He has extended his professional growth as a dyad in the PDCRT project. Roderick loves being surrounded by the thoughts, ideas, and questions of his scholars and strives to create windows in his classroom where these scholars can connect who they are and how valuable they are in order to change and grow not just within themselves but in everything the world is and will be. Roderick shares his many travels and adventures with his wife, along with their backgrounds and experiences growing up.

Northern Parkway School

The school where Alicia and Roderick teach is richly culturally, linguistically, and ethnically diverse, with a population of over 600 students, 90% of whom receive free and reduced-price meals. The majority of children and families identify as Latinx and Black. Some have immigrated recently, and most have family members from Central and South America and the Caribbean, representing many countries, including El Salvador, Jamaica, Honduras, Columbia, the Dominican Republic, and Haiti.

Kerry Elson is now in her 11th year of teaching and has been teaching in New York public schools for 6 years. Kerry, who identifies as White and able-bodied, first learned about culturally relevant, critical sociocultural, and social constructivist teaching methods as a student at Bank Street College of Education and as an assistant teacher at Bank Street School for Children, the College's laboratory school. She currently teaches kindergarten and 1st grade in a loop. When Kerry isn't teaching, she likes spending time with friends, trying new restaurants, and writing short humor pieces about guinea pigs, theater, food, and more.

Haydée Dohrn-Melendez Morgan is currently in her 18th year of teaching and has been teaching kindergarten, 1st grade, and prekindergarten in New York City public schools for 13 years. She teaches 3-year-old kindergartners and prekindergartners in a loop at a school in East Harlem, a position she has held for 4 years. Haydée, who is Puerto Rican, also considers her life's work to be laughing with her husband and riding on their motorcycle, where she is often fueled by the beauty of nature, and learning and growing as a mother of two teenage children who inspire her to be present in all moments and to notice the magic in a smile.

Central Park East 2 (CPE 2)

The school where Kerry and Haydée teach is also richly diverse in terms of language, ethnicity, and the lived experiences of the school community. Of the students at the school, 81% are of Color—about 40% Latinx, 32% Black, 7% Interracial, and 5% Asian. Each year, Kerry and Haydée's children speak many different heritage languages, including Spanish, Tagalog, Mandarin, French, Arabic, Hebrew, and African American language, among others.

Kindel Turner Nash is currently an associate professor and the Spangler Distinguished Professor of Early Childhood Literacy at Appalachian State University. Kindel is White and connected to the Black community by marriage. She was a public school teacher and literacy specialist (grades pre-K–8) in urban and Department of Defense schools for 10 years prior to becoming a teacher-educator. When Kindel isn't writing or teaching future teachers, she enjoys playing her Martin guitar with her Dad, long rambling hikes, gardening, Southern-style dinners, poetry, and discussing philosophy, religion, and history with her husband.

AN INVITATION

As noted in the opening of this chapter, we see children as people—little, full people. These little, full people merit teaching that sustains the fullness of their cultures, languages, and histories. We invite you to engage with this book as a way to ensure that children's fullness is mediated, honored, extended, and sustained in your classrooms. In this way, you might create processes and practices that build bridges between schools and the lifeworlds of Indigenous, Black, Latinx, and Asian and Pacific Islander children, families, and communities. You might teach in ways that honor the knowledge and belief that *children come full*.

CHAPTER 2

No Behavior Charts
Building Sustaining Learning Communities for Young Children

*Kindel Turner Nash, Alicia Arce-Boardman, Roderick Peele,
Kerry Elson, and Haydée Dohrn-Melendez Morgan*

One spring, a preservice teacher accompanied Kindel on a visit to the teachers' classrooms. She had been completing her student teaching internship in an urban school where color-coded behavior charts were the norm; blue and green signaled good behavior and red signaled bad behavior. After spending the entire morning observing Kerry and Haydée's classes, Kindel and the teacher candidate debriefed over lunch. The teacher candidate reflected, "I love how the classroom community is so child-centered, but I can't believe there's no behavior chart!"

Educators often toss around the phrase *classroom community*, as did the preservice teacher above. Too often, "good classroom community" means children are quiet and well-behaved, often understood according to White middle-class norms of behavior. Smith (2018) discusses this "superficial notion of community" and offers an alternative rooted in the African concept of communal love, or love that "runs deep and is grounded in the affirmation that your existence, your successes, your pain, and your wounds are all welcomed" (p. 116). Culturally sustaining pedagogies (CSPs) insist on communal love, through sustaining community practices while linking them with past and present (Paris & Alim, 2017a). Yet, schools, reflecting broader society, are often spaces that reinforce Whiteness and carceral logics as the norm, with scant evidence of honoring or extending the ways of knowing, being, and doing of Communities of Color (Beneke et al., 2022; Miller, 2015). Carceral logics are "ideas and practices that naturalize policing children's bodies, minds, and behaviors to maintain social control. Fueled by racism,

> *Focus Questions:* How can teachers build relationships and set up classrooms that create, foster, and sustain a sense of agency and belongingness? How can teachers work with children to develop procedural knowledge?

ableism, and linguicism, carceral logics position some children as inherently valuable and others as deviant" (Beneke et al., 2022, n.p.). Carceral logics are particularly prevalent in urban contexts, where standardized practices and systems of accountability often force children who do not assimilate to that norm into the school-to-prison nexus (Annamma, 2018). However, in their classrooms, Alicia, Haydée, Roderick, and Kerry strive to foster input, agency, and communal love in classrooms that link to the past and present of communities and are homes-away-from-homes (Baines et al., 2018).

Fostering communal love is also important in "reclaiming" the notion of classroom community as spaces where

> we, alongside our students [and families], develop ways of talking, thinking, interacting, and valuing one another as human beings, where things are not always easy, but they *are* dynamic, engaging, and respectful . . . a place where students [and families] get to be and become distinct individuals. (Laman, 2013, p. 10)

Doucet (2017) asks, "What does a culturally sustaining learning climate look like?" In order to create culturally sustaining classroom environments, we must envision practices that "explore, honor, extend, and at times, problematize [children's] cultural practices and investments" (Alim & Paris, 2017, p. 3). This chapter showcases the ways the teachers do just that as they reclaim communities together with families and children. This process begins well before the first day of school, through home and community visits, informal gatherings, and family interviews. These connections grow communication practices and classroom setups that foster a culturally sustaining classroom environment where children's behaviors need not be controlled via a behavior chart.

BEFORE THE SCHOOL YEAR BEGINS

Alicia, Haydée, Roderick, and Kerry know that children come to school with a whole structure that has been at play—that *children come full*. As our model depicts, the processes and practices of teaching literacy are embedded within and connected to the multiple layers of a child's lived experiences. Part of their responsibility as teachers is to understand that structure. This starts early, usually before school even begins.

Alicia distributes her cellphone number and sends introductory texts to all of the families of her students. Kerry and Haydée send families introductory emails and invite them to an informal playground gathering before the first day of school. Haydée's future students visit her classroom the preceding June to meet the teachers, see the classroom, and have their pictures taken to be placed on labels that signify that the classroom is their space. Roderick visits each of his students at home prior to the first day of school and then at least two more times throughout the school year. Rooted in notions of communal love, all of these practices negate the need for a behavior management system.

A Note About Family Communication

The teachers feel that to take care of children, you need to take care of families, in a partnership. They use a variety of ways to openly communicate with families: a laminated folder that children carry between home and school, conversations before and after school, informal and formal conferences, phone calls and texts, emails, social media posts, weekly newsletters, and get-togethers. They communicate across heritage languages based on cues they receive from families, using translation services when needed. This practice of multilingual communication reflects CSP's goal of critically centering multilingualism (Paris & Alim, 2017a). Yet, the teachers know that there is more to communication and building relationships with families than information sharing.

When the teachers make themselves accountable to families and communities, they develop *confianza*—defined as a mutual trust "which is re-established or confirmed with each exchange and leads to the development of long-term relationships" (González et al., 1993, p. 3). Roderick builds such strong relationships that previous students often return to visit. Alicia has noticed that making herself available to families outside of class and school hours erases the invisible power line between teacher, children, and families. Alicia values families' time, so they respect and value hers. Sometimes, Alicia receives quick morning phone calls from parents before school to ask about a school trip. Alicia, Roderick, Haydée, and Kerry feel that it is so important to contact families at least every other month to share something positive: maybe their child said something thoughtful at a meeting or worked particularly hard on something—they want families to share in that joy! These ways of communicating are so important, as decades of research indicates that when teachers and families are in partnership together, children's opportunities for success in schools increase (Edwards, 2016; Sanders & Epstein, 2005).

Informal Playground Gatherings

Informal playground gatherings before the school year starts help families, children, and teachers get to know one another. The gathering is simple. While not every family can attend every year because of scheduling conflicts, the teachers typically try to choose an afternoon that is close to the first day of school to increase the chances that people will be in town. Some families bring dinner and picnic in the park, as well. The conversations at this before-school gathering are informal. While sometimes families may want to engage in important discussions about their child's needs at this event, Kerry encourages families to set up a phone call with her at a later time instead so that she can devote more time and attention to the conversation. While at her family playground gathering, Haydée engages in conversations with the child's family and caretakers to create a relationship of understanding and teamwork. Families have time to ask their questions in an informal setting and share their thoughts (often including concerns) before the big first day of school.

At these gatherings, children choose how they will interact with Kerry or Haydée and their new classmates. Often when families arrive, a parent introduces their child to Kerry or Haydée, but after that, a child may want to talk or play with their teachers for a while; other times, the child may wish to play with other children or spend time on their own. Kerry and Haydée want children to interact with them and with new classmates in whatever way feels most comfortable for them. They want children to feel that their need for interaction or for personal space will be respected. They hope that if the children feel that respect, they'll be more comfortable with Kerry and Haydée and with their classmates on the first day of school.

This informal gathering helps lessen the anxiety children might feel about the first day of school. It also helps families get to know one another. The playground setting accommodates many needs: children can play, meet one another, and meet their teachers away from the school. Later, children might say, "I saw you at the park!" CSPs develop teachers' capacity to create a curriculum that constantly asks: *What do we seek to sustain? How does that influence what we decide to read, write, perform, and teach and in what classroom settings?* (Paris & Alim, 2017). Informal gatherings such as these create space and time for teachers, children, and families to explore these questions, as they think about the year ahead.

Gathering of Stories and Home Visits

The teachers believe that families are the real experts about their children. This is why they engage in gathering stories and in home visits and meetings at home or school with children and families. Through these, the teachers listen to and seek families' stories and funds of knowledge (Gonzaléz et al., 2005). The concept of funds of knowledge is rooted in Luis Moll, Norma Gonzalez, and Cathy Amanti's (1993) study of Latinx communities' ways of knowing. They define "funds of knowledge" as "the skills and knowledge that have been historically and culturally developed to enable an individual or household to function within a given culture" (p. 131).

Gathering of Stories. Gathering of stories builds on Koplow's (2002) notion of parent–teacher conferences as story-gathering. Haydée and Kerry have adapted it beyond parent–teacher conferences. Knowing the families' or caregivers' stories helps them bring children to the places where they are typically most secure. Haydée and Kerry meet each family, using questions that inspire organic conversation about the child and the family (see Figure 2.1). During gathering-of-stories visits, families discuss their child's birth, first words, friendships, and any prior school or day care experiences. Families can share whatever information they wish to. The goal is to get to know families while respecting privacy.

Figure 2.1. Gathering of Stories Questions (Adapted from Koplow, 2002)

Can you tell me more about the very beginning of your child's life? What do you remember about your child's birth?
How did you choose your child's name?
When did your child begin to crawl? Walk? How would you describe walking in these early days—adventurous? Cautious? When did your child begin to talk? What were your child's first words?
What languages does your child speak? What languages has your child been exposed to at home or in school settings?
If your child attended preschool or day care, how did your child handle separation? Was there anything your child particularly liked or disliked in those settings?
Who are the people in the child's home? Who are the important people in your child's life?
What are the most important things for me to know about your child?

Gathering of stories helps the teachers and families form bonds of trust. If families trust the teachers, then children may be more likely to trust them, as well. It is a time of learning for Haydée and Kerry that they hold sacred.

Home Visits. Roderick spends time visiting his students at home at the beginning of each school year. When he receives his classroom list, he writes to families to introduce himself and share his plans to visit. He approaches this home visit with the following questions, but really, he wants to share his focus on equity, and engage in open-ended discussion about children's learning paths and cultural backgrounds or areas of needed support. Questions he asks during home visits include:

- Tell me about your cultural, ethnic, and/or language background and how you would like to see that in the classroom.
- What are your goals for your child this year?
- What support do you feel your child needs this year?

During the pandemic, Roderick has used Google Meet to do these visits, but he has found that the virtual format is not as effective, even if it is necessary during such times. He finds that families do not want to be on camera, have trouble arranging their schedule, and do not seem to view these as important in the same way as they do face-to-face home visits. While all these are very understandable given the multiple challenges during the pandemic, Roderick prefers and recommends in-person home visits whenever possible. Other tools for developing deep understanding about children and communities include the Reflective–Inquiry–Questioning (RIQ) Learner Inventory, Class, and Community Profiles (Hollins, 2015a, 2019). These tools help preservice and inservice teachers understand the school context and local community and get to know children and families.

Alicia also forms very close relationships with children and families. While Alicia's life doesn't permit her to visit every child, she is in constant, close contact with all families through text-message, phone, and quick home visits. By being responsive and spending time with and collecting the stories of children and families, Haydée, Roderick, Alicia, and Kerry are able to place children and their families' funds of knowledge at the center of every aspect of their teaching. CSPs seek to move beyond viewing heritage, cultural, and community practices as static cultural resources to be "considered" in the classroom. Instead, CSPs look at the dynamic ways cultural and linguistic practices are constantly shifting and evolving (Paris & Alim, 2014). Once they have engaged with families' dynamic stories, they use those foundational understandings and stories to set up their classroom spaces.

SETTING UP THE CLASSROOM

Ideally, the teachers want their classrooms to be spaces that sustain "the lifeways of communities who have been and continue to be damaged and erased through schooling" (Alim & Paris, 2017, p. 1). This starts by ensuring that the classroom is simple and bare. In the first weeks of school, very little adorns the walls except name tags or photos for each child on a bulletin board, cubbies, and tables/desks. This will change. As if moving into a new home, the classroom will be created and adorned with what is important to children as they begin to claim it. Their simple rooms convey *possibility*: a room waiting to hold them and all their ideas and work.

Before the school year begins, the teachers create and label core areas. These include: (a) meeting spaces for share time, dancing, and whole-group instruction, (b) vibrant culturally and linguistically authentic classroom libraries, (c) seating areas with furniture arrangements that frame particular areas for small groups to work, and (d) spaces for choice time. While each classroom has these core elements, the setups look different because of the age of the children and the school/community context. These spaces form a sort of third space, where children can engage in dynamic, agentic learning (Adair, 2014). Third spaces are "functional systems whose division of labor, tools, and practices are oriented toward expansive forms of learning and powerful literacies" (Gutiérrez & Johnson, 2017, pp. 252–253). A diagram of Kerry's classroom displays these four common classroom areas (see Figure 2.2).

Meeting Spaces

The meeting spaces in each classroom are physical and emotional centering points where children gather, multiple times a day, in a circle, to share their stories and lives. Smith (2018) discusses the symbolic power of a circle: "within the circle, hearts and spirits are vulnerably open; ensuring that all who sit or stand in a circle are heard and valued and healed"(pp. 118–119).

Figure 2.2. Classroom Diagram

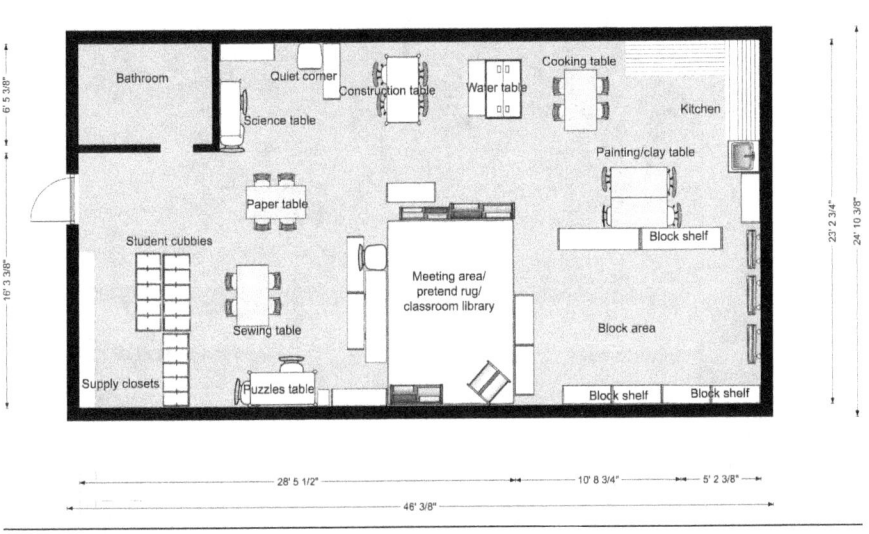

In Alicia's classroom, the meeting area is created by a colorful carpet flanked on three sides by a Smartboard, Alicia's desk, and a chart stand holding books. Roderick's meeting area is where children have the opportunity to dance to hip-hop and salsa music during periodic dance breaks. Kerry's meeting area is a bright blue carpet surrounded by low shelving. Haydée's bright rug is placed front and center in the classroom, with circular disks with children's names placed in a circle (see Figure 2.3). Informal talk and sharing in the meeting areas centers "dynamic practices and selves of students" (Alim & Paris, 2017, p. 3).

Classroom Library

Books promote connections and unity (Baldwin, 1993). The teachers create connections through classroom libraries that contain books that reflect students' languages, cultures, and interests and support criticality. They know they must do more than merely "adding some books about people of color" (Ladson-Billings, 2014, p. 82). Understanding that "educational transformation cannot occur with . . . a white-washing of literature or wrapping ourselves in the myth of [color-evasiveness]" (Smith, 2018, p. 118), they want classroom libraries to become fodder for transformation. To promote not just unity but linguistic and racial justice (Baker-Bell, 2020).

Book Selection. All of the teachers select books that reflect their students' and families' home languages. Kerry and Haydeé, for example, include books in their libraries by bilingual authors, such as Angela Dominguez and Monica

Figure 2.3. Preschool Meeting Area

Brown. Alicia's library contains many Spanish books. Several principles guide book selection (Boutte, 2002); the teachers select books that:

1) Feature main characters who are Black, Brown, and Indigenous,
2) Feature a variety of languages and language varieties,
3) Feature main characters who are disabled,
4) Feature main characters who self-identify as LGBTQIA,

and,

5) Are written and illustrated by insider-members of the community.

The Lee and Low Books (2017) Classroom Library questionnaire can be helpful for evaluating and creating this kind of classroom library. It took time for the teachers to build their carefully curated collections, but through grants, school funds, and crowdsourcing, the teachers have been able to build robust classroom libraries.

Roderick feels that it's important to select topics and stories that introduce scholars to storylines that they can connect to. Roderick does this by asking families to lend books to his library at the beginning of the year.

Roderick loves to see children's reactions when he adds books in Spanish, Haitian-Creole, French, Mandarin, Yoruba, Twi, and Arabic. When scholars ask, "Why do you have these?" he responds, "We have people in the class that read these languages!"

The teachers also select books based on children's interests. Reflecting children's and families' concerns at the start of the year—Haydée selects and reads books about coming and going, beginning and ending, and families, including *Please, Baby, Please* by Spike Lee and Tonya Lewis Lee, *The Kissing Hand* by Audrey Penn, and *Owl Babies* by Martin Wadell. Kerry and Haydée also choose books to display during the first weeks of school based on what they learned about children's interests during the before-school playground gathering. For example, one year Kerry learned that several children were excited about losing their first teeth over the summer, so she added books about losing teeth from different cultural perspectives, such as *I lost My Tooth in Africa* by Penda Diakite, *The Tooth Fairy Meets El Ratón Pérez* by René Colato Laínez, and *I Lost My Tooth!* by Mo Willems, to the classroom library for children to read during the first weeks of school.

Displaying Books. Haydée places books on two large display-style bookshelves. When teaching 3-K, she puts only board books in the library until she becomes familiar with children's ability to handle books. When her students from 3-K return for pre-K, she makes sure to place favorite 3-K texts in the classroom library so children can rekindle the deep connection they cultivated during the previous school year. In pre-K, children can choose a book to take from the library each day to take home to read. Haydée also makes sure to read aloud all of the books that are placed in the classroom library to build children's familiarity and connection with the texts. Children who are 3 and 4 years old often read the texts by memory, which is an important phase of reading development.

Alicia's library is not confined to one corner of the class—every inch bursts with book baskets and texts. Her students know that they have access to all of the books in the classroom. Kerry's library flanks her meeting area. Roderick's library spans the entire back wall of his classroom (see Figure 2.4). Kerry and Roderick both involve children in labeling the book baskets of themed books that make up their classroom libraries, which you will read more about in later chapters (Nash et al., 2019).

Seating Areas

All of the teachers create seating areas to support small-group collaboration, which develops agency and negates the need to control behavior (Adair, 2014). In Alicia's class, desks are grouped together in clusters of four or five. Similarly, Roderick's students sit at five round tables. Most tables in Kerry's room seat two to four children. Kerry knows that in big groups, the noise level can be distracting, so she rarely has tables for more than four. Children

Figure 2.4. Roderick's Classroom Library

often use these seating areas for different purposes. In Kerry's class, the tables and areas of the room are primarily set up for work time (see the next section), but children also use them for independent work. Additionally, they sit at the tables for snack time and use them as a home base for unpacking and packing up. In addition to seats at tables, comfy beach chairs, placemats, disks, dog beds, and beanbag chairs are available to children as they work independently or together throughout the day.

Assigning Seats. Alicia, Roderick, Kerry, and Haydée take varied approaches to assigning seats, basing their decisions on what they think might benefit their students. In Alicia's class, there is no assigned seating. In her classroom, more importance is put on what children are learning, how they are learning, and who they are learning and talking with. Meanwhile, Roderick, Haydée, and Kerry do assign seats to help students work with a variety of peers. Roderick groups students so that they have opportunities to interact and cooperatively work with peers with different skills, abilities, and talents. Kerry assigns children seats at a particular table based on what she has observed about how they work best. Kerry changes the seating arrangements a few times a year to help children work with different classmates and try different work environments. If a child seems to focus better at a table for two, Kerry will make sure they sit at one of those tables. Through these kinds of seating arrangements, Alicia, Roderick, Haydée, and Kerry place value on their students' repertoires of practice—that is, "the ways of engaging in activities stemming from participation in a range of cultural practices, as well as the learning that occurs in the development of those repertoires" (Gutiérrez & Johnson, 2017, p. 251). They see inherent dignity in their students' everyday talk, and so they foster both independence and interdependence through their seating configurations.

Spaces for Choice Time

Choice time (otherwise known as free play, center time, or work time) furthers children's development of self-understanding within social, cultural, collaborative arenas (Dyson, 2013; Vygotsky, 1978). When building collaboratively, Legos become bridges between past and present communities. Blocks become skyscraping hotels with child-created billboards that say: "Best hotl in the wold." These spaces can be culturally sustaining—facilitating children's connections to histories of families and communities, of cities, and of nation-states (Paris & Alim, 2017a).

While her school and curriculum do not include daily choice play time, Alicia creates communal spaces for children to engage with Legos, playdough, and paper every Friday. Roderick has two daily opportunities for choice play. During this time, his students may get together in a book club; read independently; write in their thinking notebook; or relax, draw, and eat their daily snack.

Haydée and Kerry's daily choice time is called "work time." During daily work time, children choose to pretend play, build with blocks, construct creatively with found objects, play in water or sand, paint, cook, work with paper or clay, sew, and more. Some years, there's also a science table with a snail tank and a worm bin or a music lab or puzzles station. Haydée and Kerry arrange their rooms to create work-time areas. They both set aside as much room as they can for a block area on one side of the room. In Kerry's classroom, on the big rug where they have morning meeting, children can build with large hollow blocks and use fabric and other accessories for pretend playing. In other spots in both Haydée and Kerry's rooms, there are nooks for puzzles, painting, cooking, and building with reusable materials like cardboard boxes and bottle caps. Year after year, when Kindel visits, the children at CPE 2 tell her, "Work time is my favorite part of the day!" Work time can be a kind of alternate, or *third space,* where children develop a "new social imagination in which they can engage in historicized, sociocritical, and syncretic processes of reframing their cultural past as a resource in the present and a tool for future action" (Gutiérrez & Johnson, 2017, pp. 252–253).

Through getting to know children before the school year even begins, the teachers are able to create classroom spaces that bridge home and school. Additionally, the way the teachers physically set up their classrooms creates inviting and engaging spaces where children can be seen and heard and where children's multilingual and multicultural heritage and community practices are critically centered (Paris & Alim, 2017). Building children's understanding about how to *belong* in these communal classroom spaces, the teachers create rules/norms, routines, and celebrations and introduce strategies to resolve conflicts. In this way, they are focused on building classroom communities with children rather than managing children within classrooms.

NORMS, ROUTINES, CONFLICTS, AND CELEBRATIONS

Kinloch (2017) notes that in order for CSPs to be effective, teachers need to foster collaborative, collective, critical, and loving environments that support cultural identities. On a poster at her son's school, Alicia recently read the words: "If a child doesn't know how to read, we teach them to read. If a child doesn't know how to swim, we teach them to swim. If a child doesn't know how to be part of a classroom community, we need to teach them how to, but instead, we punish them." These words embody the way the teachers feel about the importance of establishing classroom rules or norms, routines, and jobs.

As the teachers create norms and routines, children develop the procedural knowledge necessary to be part of such environments. Procedural knowledge involves the "principles and rules that provide direction for performing cognitive activities" (Hollins, 2015a, p. 154). Since culture and language influence mental processes, developing procedural knowledge fosters spaces that support cultural identities (Hollins, 2015a). For example, when communicating with her bilingual students, Alicia sometimes leads with Spanish, sometimes with English, and sometimes translanguages across multiple languages and language varieties to "maximize communicative potential" (García, 2009, p. 140). Each teacher enacts very different practices and routines relevant to their local contexts and the needs of their particular students.

Community Agreements and Expectations

The three pillars of Alicia and Roderick's school are responsibility, respectfulness, and caring. Every single morning, especially in the beginning, Alicia and Roderick remind children that they need to embody these pillars. They ask questions like "What does responsibility look like? What does respectfulness look like? What does it mean to be caring?" Children often respond with thoughts like "I have to use a low voice so I don't disrupt my classmates" or "I have to get my work done."

Neither Roderick nor Alicia posts classroom rules and expectations or community agreements; they typically build agreements about their expectations based on the pillars and thought-provoking quotes. Alicia carefully selects quotes based on her knowledge of the community surrounding the school and her desire to foster interdependence and *confianza* (González et al., 1993). Quotes include *Ser bilngue es un super poder/Being bilingual is a superpower; Stories Matter, Many Stories Matter* (Chimamanda Adichie); *Live Your Best Life*; and *When they go low, we go High* (Michelle Obama). In Roderick's class, the verbs *Learn, Read, Write,* and *Create* run the perimeter of the room. Roderick talks with the children about what these words mean, and they discuss how they can work together to make the classroom a place where these verbs can be put into action. Roderick is the kind of teacher who students don't want to disappoint. He is respectful and caring and understands students at a deep level. He also gets to know families well and builds solid relationships with them. These actions help him create an ethic of caring (Noddings, 2012) in his classroom. Children seem to feel like that they are in a relationship with Roderick. How could they not, when in every interaction Roderick communicates that he cares?

The very beginning of school is set up with half-day classes for Haydée's pre-K class, allowing time for children to bond with adults and work into the full day of school. They spend a chunk of their mornings outside, where Haydée guides children as they negotiate needs and wants that arise in the work of playing. When children need guidance, they take playground walks with her. As she links children's physical and mental actions to their cultural and historical settings (Gregory et al., 2004) (the playground), she establishes one of the most important community agreements of pre-K, "Keep one another safe." In this way, she helps children negotiate their needs and wants as they share in "a joint culture between teacher and child" (Gregory et al., 2004, pp. 8–9).

For Kerry, the word *rule* can have negative associations with compliance. Instead, she centers children in the creation of community agreements building on their input (Paris & Alim, 2017a). Kerry and the children begin creating their overarching classroom community agreements in the first couple of weeks of school. She starts by asking:

- "What is school for?"
- "Why are we coming here five days a week?"
- "How do you want to feel at school?"

These questions help establish children's goals for being at school. One year, in response to the question "How do you want to feel at school?"

children said that they wanted to feel "happy" and "smart." Kerry writes their responses down and presents them to children later to help think together about what they need to do so everyone can reach these goals. Next, she asks children about why they have rules at home. Often students might say, "It's something you have to do," or "I can't argue with my brother." After they have established goals for school and a basic understanding of rules in general, they brainstorm and interactively write class agreements (this process is similar to one Kerry has learned about from the Center for Responsive Schools).

After brainstorming about goals for school and the general purpose of rules, Kerry and the children condense their list into three to five basic community agreements. In kindergarten, next to each big rule, she writes down the smaller ways to follow that rule, adding photos of children doing that action. In 1st grade, Kerry and children interactively write the rules and everyone signs their names in agreement (see Figure 2.5).

Privileging children in the creation of community agreements and expectations fosters collectivity and community accountability (Alim & Paris, 2017; Kinloch, 2017), creating an alternative to the need to manage children's behavior. The same care that the teachers take in creating community agreements is taken in creating classroom schedules and routines.

Figure 2.5. Community Agreements in Kindergarten and 1st Grade

(continued)

No Behavior Charts 27

Figure 2.5. *(continued)*

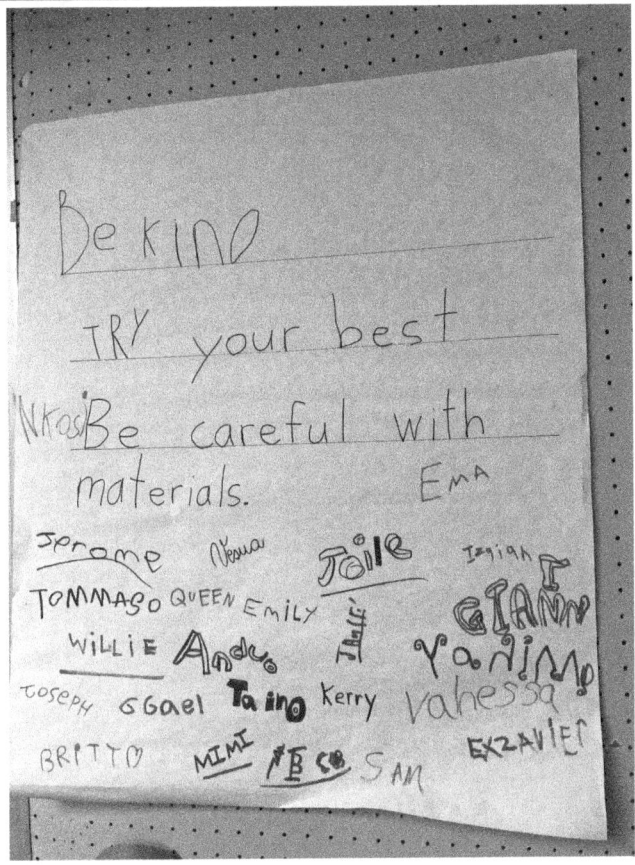

Classroom Schedule and Routines

Each teacher creates and prominently posts a classroom schedule that they gradually introduce (see Table 2.1). Haydée's schedule is displayed from left to right so that children can work on directionality (see bottom of bulletin board in Figure 2.3).

Routines

Just as they work with their students to build collective understandings about the procedural knowledge necessary to be in a community together, the teachers carefully teach routines. To do so, they might start by asking children why they might do a particular routine in the classroom or why a routine is important. For example, they might ask: "Why do we walk on line? Why do we have meetings? Why do we unpack? Why do we push in chairs?" The teachers want children to know the purpose of classroom routines and feel

Table 2.1. Classroom Schedules

Alicia (2/3)	Roderick (2)	Haydée (Pre-K)	Kerry (K/1)
8:20–8:30 Unpacking	*8:10–8:20* Dropoff	*8:20–8:30* Dropoff	*8:20–8:30* Unpacking
8:30–8:45 Morning meeting	*8:20–8:40* Morning meeting	*8:30–9:00* Breakfast	*8:30–8:45* Morning meeting
8:45–9:00 Read-aloud	*8:40–9:00* Choice time	*9:00–9:15* Morning meeting	*8:45–9:15* Reading/word work
9:00–10:40 Guided reading	*9:00–9:30* Word work	*9:15–10:35* Outdoor play/ Specials	*9:15–10* Math
10:40–12:15 Lunch/ Specials	*9:35–10:35* Math	*10:35–10:50* Snack	*10–10:50* Work time
12:15–1:10 Math	*10:40–11:40* Reading/ writing	*10:50–11:50* Work time	*10:50–noon* Lunch/ Specials
1:10–2:10 Writing/ integrated science/ social studies/ choice time	*11:40–noon* Choice time	*11:50–noon* Read-aloud	*12–12:15* Kindness meeting
2:10–2:15 Snack	*Noon–2:00* Lunch/ Specials	*12:00–1:30* Rest	*12:15–1:50* Writing
2:15–2:35 Closing meeting	*2:00–2:40* Social studies	*1:30–2:15* Choice	*1:50–2:05* Read-aloud
	2:40–2:50 Closing cipher	*2:15–2:35* Closing meeting	*2:05–2:25* Snack, packing up, reading
			2:25–2:35 Closing meeting

that if the ideas arise from the children and they are involved in establishing the routine's purpose, they may feel more invested in following steps for a routine. Once they establish a routine's purpose, they talk about how to follow the steps of a routine. Roderick and Kerry also teach the students ways to nonverbally communicate, such as a bathroom signal or signals of agreement and disagreement. When children follow certain routines, the teachers feel that those routines are more calm, more organized, and take up less time, allowing more time for learning. For that reason, they work with students to practice routines in many, many different ways. Some examples of routines that are practiced over and over again include how to work independently, how to get set up for different instructional time periods, how to clean up, and how to transition in and out of the room. Within all of these clear guidelines, there is freedom. All of the teachers want children to have enough structure that they feel secure, but they also want to leave enough room for children to interpret tasks in different ways based on their own social and cultural knowledge and feelings (Koplow, 2021). By allowing for freedom within a larger structure, the teachers hope children will feel that their languages, community practices, interests, feelings, and needs are welcome and that they belong in the classroom.

Creating Classroom Jobs

Similar to other culturally sustaining beginning-of-the-year practices described so far, the need for classroom jobs arises from a sense of responsibility to reclaim spaces where children "see, hear, and feel their worth . . . where the classroom becomes a home away from home" (Baines et al., 2018, p. 62). Roderick's class doesn't have assigned jobs; instead he fosters collectivity and communalism by encouraging everyone to help. Alicia, Kerry, and Haydée's classes co-create jobs with children and have a chart that shows who is doing each job. Sometimes Kerry and Haydée may casually ask a child to help set up snack or water plants or feed the snails. At the beginning of the year, children may see the teacher always doing particular tasks and they'll say, "Could I do that?" When these questions come up, they show children a job chart. They want the chart to result from a natural need, so that children understand why they have classroom jobs and a job chart. This job chart is structured about the same each year, but the jobs themselves vary from year to year, depending on ideas the children have suggested and the needs of each particular group (see Figure 2.6).

Figure 2.6. Job Chart

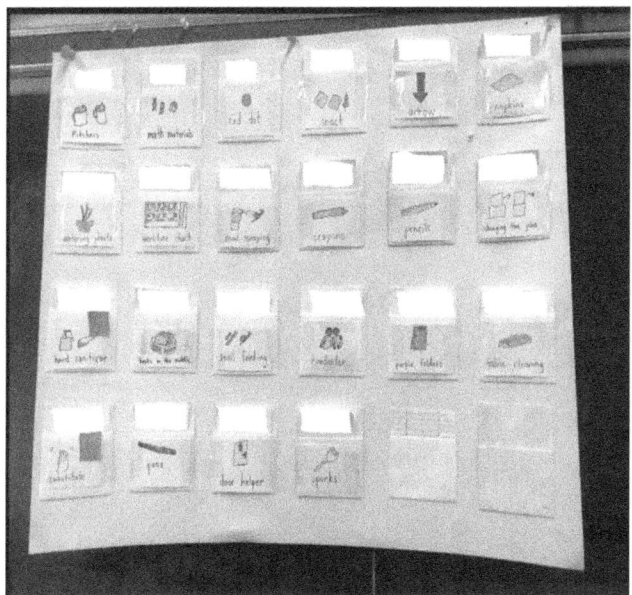

Resolving Conflicts: Kindness as Justice

Kindness is a touchstone to resolving conflicts within classroom communities; teaching about kindness alone, as individual acts, is not enough. It must go right alongside teaching justice.

Kindness as justice means singing happy birthday to your friends in their chosen language, even though it sounds different from yours. It means teaching into the moment when some children say, "You are not pretty, your skin is too dark" by engaging with books like *I Am Enough* by Grace Byers, about the beauty of Blackness and Brownness. Alicia fosters an understanding of kindness as justice by spending time at the beginning of the year discussing with children the concept of tolerance. She shares books that she feels will help children reflect on the concept of kindness as justice. Some of the books she shares with her class include *Each Kindness* by Jacqueline Woodson, *The Sandwich Swap* by Queen Rania Al Abdullah of Jordan and Kelly DiPucchio, *The Story of Ruby Bridges* by Robert Cole, or *Salam Alaikum: A Measure of Peace* by Harris J. These books deal with how teachers and children handle social rejection and navigate cultural and racial differences in school. She then asks children to discuss instances in these stories where people were hurt and how people could have been kind, tolerant, responsible, respectful, and caring (connecting back to the school's pillars) instead.

Kerry holds "Kindness Meetings," where each child talks about something or someone that was kind, or "Friendship Snack," where children write a note and draw a picture for a classmate to share during snack (see Figure 2.7). Children place their note at the recipient's table spot and then they eat their snack. Kerry turns the lights low, puts electric tea lights on tables, and plays quiet music. Children enjoy reading each other's notes and often take them home to save. Generally, during this friendship snack, there's a warm, positive feeling in the room. Even as challenges inevitably arise in

Figure 2.7. Friendship Snack Letter

the group, Kerry ensures that there is this time to reconnect and revisit their shared value of being kind to one another. These practices create spaces that sustain "minds and bodies" (Alim & Paris, 2017, p. 13).

Resolving Conflicts

Teaching children the necessary social skills and practices to resolve conflicts enables "living, learning, and working together in harmony with solidarity" (Hollins, 2019, p. 62). When children understand how to resolve the inevitable conflicts that arise, their behavior does not need to be controlled by the teacher. For example, Alicia finds that the *confianza* she fosters helps to mediate conflicts. When Alicia sees disagreements arise in her classroom, she encourages children to work out their problems with one another. She also finds that if she has a particular student who is acting out, giving that student a special job can help redirect that child's energy in a more positive direction.

Roderick and Alicia's school uses a restorative justice approach to solving conflicts (see Restorative Practices: A Guide for Educators, Schott Foundation at http://schottfoundation.org/restorative-practices for more information). This approach engages children in thinking about repairing situations in which they have hurt someone. In Roderick's class, when someone has been harmed, he brings the class family together in a *cipher,* a practice rooted in African and Indigenous traditions (Hill & Petchauer, 2013). In this communal cipher, grounded in the school values of being respectful, responsible, and caring, the "harmed" person talks about what happened using the following restorative practice questions as a guide:

- What happened? What's been happening?
- What were you thinking while this was happening?
- What have you been thinking about since then?
- What do you think needs to happen now to make this right?
- How can we involve everyone who has been affected in finding a way forward?
- How can everyone do things differently in the future?

Then the harmed person and the person who harmed talk together about how they can resolve the conflict and repair the harm to the person who was offended/hurt. Others in the cipher can add their thoughts. Roderick and Alicia's school also has a "conflict resolution zone" outside, where kids and adults can work together to resolve conflicts.

Sentence stems can provide young children with tools for resolving conflicts. Kerry teaches children sentence stems like: "I feel . . . when you . . . could you . . . ?" to help them solve problems. If a child wants to join a game and another child denies them, they could say, "I feel upset when you say I can't play. Could you please let me play?" She has found that children can use these simple phrases in almost any situation. Of course they don't have to say these exact words, but in her experience, children are sometimes unsure of how to solve a problem on their own and what to say; they seem relieved to know that they can start by saying simple phrases. Kerry teaches children these phrases at a meeting, often with puppets, and also makes anchor charts with these sentence stems and supplies books describing typical classroom conflicts. Kerry reads these books with children during a meeting. Then she places the books in the classroom library. After reading about each sample conflict, she asks the children how the characters might solve the problem using the "I feel" words, as they have come to call them. When problems arise, Kerry asks children to try solving problems first on their own with these phrases and if they still aren't sure how to resolve the issue, she is happy to help.

Celebrations

Alicia, Roderick, Haydée, and Kerry have each developed special ways to commemorate birthdays. Roderick even has a crown children can wear on their birthday! Typically, Roderick and Alicia reach out to families at the beginning of the school year to find out if there are any customary ways that families honor birthdays. If families engage in specific cultural traditions around birthdays, Roderick and Alicia invite those families into the classroom to share their traditions. For example, one year a family from Jamaica shared that the birthday person chooses someone to cut their birthday cake together with them. Even though they do not eat cake and candy at Alicia and Roderick's school, they have found food substitutes like fruit platters or pupusas, a thick, griddle pancake originating from El Salvador and Honduras, to share on these special days. Roderick's class sings Stevie Wonder's "Happy Birthday" and discusses how it was part of a decades-long effort to establish Martin Luther King Jr.'s birthday as a national holiday (King National Holiday, 1986).

In Kerry and Haydée's class, a child's family member typically comes to the class at a time that is convenient for them, and shows four to six photos of the child as he/she was growing up and tells stories about the photos. The child also can share information about the photos. After looking at photos, the class asks questions about the birthday child as he/she was growing up. The children feel connected to each other when they learn that they have something in common.

Kerry's class also typically sings happy birthday to the birthday child. The child chooses which song he/she would like to sing; children in her class know birthday songs in many languages, so they might sing a song in English, Spanish, French, Mandarin, or Italian (Elson, 2019). Choosing which song they will sing is another opportunity for children to share part of their home lives with one another. Alicia, Roderick, Haydée, and Kerry's celebrations of birthdays are more than a mere "honoring" of children's birthday traditions. They create humanizing and sustaining spaces to explore with children the differences in aspects of their identities.

CONCLUSION

The beginning of this chapter detailed the awe a preservice teacher in Kindel's class expressed as she spent time in the teachers' classrooms. In her field experiences, the preservice teacher had become accustomed to the problematic norm in many urban school settings—a focus on policing the minds and bodies of children (Beneke et al., 2022; DeVries & Zan, 2012). Having become used to managing children and controlling their behavior through the use of a behavior chart, she couldn't imagine how children could move in and out of the agentic, imaginative, creative work she saw without a silencing and compliance tool (Beneke, 2019). In contrast, this chapter has detailed the ways the teachers nurture classroom communities as communal, loving places that sustain children's fullness. We have shared multiple beginning-of-the-year culturally sustaining language and literacy practices that support the valued lifeways of communities: critically centering multilingualism in communication practices and in setting up the classroom library; building on and extending the dynamic ways of being, funds of knowledge, and histories of families and communities through gathering of stories, home visits, and informal before-school gatherings; and fostering communal love through creating community agreements, routines, ways to solve conflicts, and celebrations. As you work to reclaim classroom communities rooted in communal love, you can build a liberating, life-affirming literacy community yourself. And perhaps, there will be no need for a behavior chart.

CHAPTER 3

Sustaining Beginnings
Literacy Practices to Foster Knowing and Being Known

Kindel Turner Nash, Alicia Arce-Boardman, Roderick Peele, and Kerry Elson

One day Kerry read Derrick Barnes and Gordon James's book *I Am Every Good Thing* to her 1st-grade class. Before reading, they looked at the red cover depicting a backpack-wearing boy and thought about the title and the book. One Black child said "I think the boy looks confident." A boy who is Chinese agreed. Then a White girl said, "I think he looks angry." The Black boy disagreed. As they read, another White girl said, "I don't think the boy is being that nice." And then she said, "He makes me feel bad." Kerry responded, "Did the boy say that he thinks he's better than other people?" The girl said, "No, it just feels like that."

Kerry Roderick and Alicia teach children from many linguistic, racial, ethnic, and other backgrounds. The teachers want all of their students to feel that *they are every good thing*—that their humanness will be respected and sustained each day of school. But as the story above shows, children readily internalize the White gaze that is pervasive in our society. Why did the White girls react so negatively to the confidence and joy the boy exhibited in the book? Did just the sense that a Black boy is feeling good about himself feel like a threat? When the girls reacted that way, it reminded Kerry that some people have a knee-jerk response to the Black Lives Matter movement. "What about my life? Does it matter?" They feel that proclaiming that Black Lives Matter means you only care about Black lives. However, one

> ***Focus Questions:*** How do teachers set the stage for culturally sustaining early literacy instruction at the beginning of the year?

in every four Black men experiences police harassment or violence (Schwartz & Jahn, 2020). Black Chicagoans are 650% more likely to be murdered by police (Schwartz & Jahn, 2020). Knowing these realities, the teachers feel a great sense of responsibility to create a sense of *knowingness* through the literacy practices they use in their classrooms. At the beginning of the year, this involves more than surface-level, getting-to-know-you activities, but involves creating a space for children to understand and critique themselves as members of a complex society.

Creating knowingness requires a deep understanding of children, informed by their histories, languages, cultures, families, and communities. Building from the foundational ways teachers create communities noted in Chapter 1, this chapter showcases culturally sustaining beginning-of-the-year literacy practices: morning meetings and share times; labeling the classroom; creating identity texts; sharing read-alouds; and establishing word work, reading, and writing foundations. Grounded in the teachers' beliefs about *knowingness,* these practices ensure that children feel seen, heard, and known, creating culturally sustaining beginnings to the school year.

FOSTERING KNOWINGNESS THROUGH MORNING MEETINGS

Morning meetings (or any class meeting, for that matter) create space for dialogue and belonging. Each of the teachers' classroom day starts with a morning meeting (see Table 3.1). Alicia, Roderick, and Kerry make conscious efforts to elevate children's voices through these 15–20-minute meetings. The meetings typically involve:

1) a multilingual greeting and message,
2) open dialogue and sharing, and
3) preparing for the day ahead.

Roderick describes how when he first started conducting morning meetings, he tried out every activity from *The Morning Meeting Book* (Kriete & Davis, 2014). As a Black man wearing a self-described fly suit, he didn't feel like the practices in that book matched his African-centric style. Now, his meetings go beyond traditional and scripted approaches to incorporate African-centric methods, such as music, rhythm, and ciphers. Ciphers involve people interacting in a circular fashion and sharing ideas. The practice of forming a cipher to come together to share and to celebrate and honor voices, ideas, and stories connects to African and Indigenous familial and communal practices (Emdin, 2013).

Table 3.1. Morning Meeting in Three Classrooms

Alicia	Roderick	Kerry
• Multilingual greeting • Student-created and read morning message (rotating) • Game • Sharing about out-of-school experiences	• Greeting • Sharing music • School mantra • Weather forecast • Sharing time (thinking notebooks) • Informal conversations and discussions • Taking attendance	• Singing • Multilingual greeting (song, dance, handshake) • Share responses to a question posed in morning message • Count the number of days in school • Interactively read and write morning message

Alicia's morning meeting starts with multilingual greetings (all names in this book are pseudonyms):

Yasmine to Jennifer: ¡Hola! Jennifer, ¿Cómo estás?
Jennifer to Yasmine, and then to Jorge: ¡Hola! Yasmine, I am fine. ¡Hola! Jorge, ¿Cómo estás?

Then, they read a morning message, talk informally, and/or play a game. At the beginning of the year they often play Two Truths and a Lie. In this game, each person shares a greeting and then two truths and one lie about themselves. The rest of the class has to try and discern truths from untruths. Alicia's students rotate as authors of the multilingual morning message, which contains important information about the day. One day a child wrote: *buenos dias, suprsters toda is the 17 day. Toda we have sciencemusic.* Alicia does not expect students to spell correctly when they write the morning message—the goal is communication. This is a space where multilingualism and trusting relationships are centered. Children know that if Alicia asks them, "¿Cómo fue su noche?"/"How was your night?" during the morning meeting, she really means it.

Roderick starts his morning meeting by sharing music—songs like *Good Morning* by Cee Lo Green create an upbeat energy to start the day. Music is prominent in Roderick's teaching—it is one of the ways he historicizes content within the valued musical traditions of the community (Paris & Alim, 2017). Roderick and the children then read the school mantra "I am respectful. I am responsible. I am caring." This helps build a sense of the school values. During Roderick's morning meeting, children also share entries from their thinking notebooks (see Figure 3.9, later in this chapter).

Kerry starts her morning meetings by singing a variety of songs as children unpack; children then greet one another, count the days in school, and read a multilingual morning message. The message often includes a prompt for discussion, such as, "¡Hola! What did you do with your family this weekend?" Kerry also integrates reading, writing, and phonics work into the meeting. They sing rhyming songs or sing and clap the syllables in their names. They find the high-frequency words that they're learning about, such as "the" and "is" in the message. She also leaves places in a sentence blank so they can interactively write the words together. To do this, Kerry asks the children to count the sounds in some message words with her, and then she asks one child at a time to say the first sound they heard and the letter for that sound, then the next sound and the letter for it, and so on. As each child tells Kerry the sound and corresponding letter, she writes the letter in the message until they've written the whole word.

SHARE TIME

Share time is a dialogic practice in which classmates briefly share ideas or creations (e.g., writing, family artifacts). Share time can be incorporated into morning meetings, but it can also be part of other classroom routines, such as writing workshop. At the beginning of the year, Roderick often shares family photos during morning meeting share time. Children also share book responses from their thinking notebooks (see Figure 3.9, later in this chapter). For example, one morning, Djene shared a response to a book she had read about vultures. Following the share, others offered questions, comments, or connections:

> *Arturo:* Thank you for sharing. I have a question. What was your book mainly about?
> *Djene:* My book was mainly about vulture poop!
> *Class:* Laughter.

As children share, they often notice that they have similar ideas and experiences and start to form bonds.

At the beginning of the year, morning meeting and share times involve a lot of practice. As the year goes on, students move toward more complex ways of interacting and sharing and take ownership of the meeting. By going beyond traditional and scripted meetings and shares, the teachers are able to engage student and community input and critically center students and their communities (Paris & Alim, 2017a).

KNOWINGNESS THROUGH NAMING: LABELING THE CLASSROOM

Naming and labeling the classroom is one way to create classroom environments that are humanizing and sustaining (Doucet, 2017; Laman, 2013). During the first weeks of school, Alicia, Roderick, and Kerry label some

Figure 3.1. Teacher-Created Classroom Label

containers for materials so that children know where things belong (see Figure 3.1). Kerry also writes children's names on their cubbies and other places so that they can see how to write their names—she wants them to be able to look at a clear, neatly written model. Alicia handwrites labels in Spanish and English, privileging Spanish.

In each of the classrooms, children help write and draw multilingual labels for book baskets in the classroom library and other areas. For example, Kerry's students create labels for the cubbies where they place their class stuffed bears, one labeled "BlueBarry shaRk." As teachers open up classroom labeling to children, they find that children independently create labels of their own. For example, a child created the label "No strangors," while playing with blocks during work time (see Figure 3.2).

Figure 3.2. Child-Created Labels

KNOWINGNESS THROUGH THE CLASSROOM LIBRARY

Chapter 2 discussed in detail how the teachers set up, select, and display texts within their classroom libraries. The next section describes how the teachers foster knowingness through involving children in the setup and labeling of libraries. Alicia and Roderick create clear labels for their classroom library book baskets. Their libraries are staged to catch children's attention. On the first day, Roderick eagerly looks to see if children's heads turn to the library. However, Kerry does not label the library book baskets; instead she wants children to create those labels.

CHILD-CREATED BOOK-BASKET LABELS

Kerry has found that if children make the book-basket labels for the classroom library, they better understand where the books belong. Within the first few weeks of school, they create at least one label for a book basket during morning meeting. In kindergarten, first Kerry collects all the books that she wants to have in the library in baskets, grouped by topic or author. It feels natural because after a couple of days of independent reading, children begin to realize they can't find a book they were looking for, or they're not sure where to put a book when they're done. She might start with a basket of books all about animals. She will hold up three or four books from that basket and ask "How are they the same?" Once they come up with a name that includes all of those books (like "animals"), Kerry writes the word on a piece of paper and asks a child to draw a picture of an animal above the word during work time. Over the next several days, Kerry and her class label more baskets, until all have a label. As she adds other baskets to the classroom library throughout the year, she invites children to make other labels, and as they learn to write words on their own, they label using words.

In 1st grade, Kerry also starts the year by having book baskets in the library already in baskets grouped by category—books about teeth, animals, families, and so on. By 1st grade, children are more adept at figuring out how all the books in a basket are the same and at coming up with a name or title. They can do this work without as much support from Kerry. Kerry then asks each child to work with a partner to write labels for the basket and the shelf. Creating book-basket labels centers "rich and innovative linguistic, literate, and cultural practices" of "noticing, naming, and writing" (Paris & Alim, 2014, p. 86). She centers their voices by engaging children in democratic discussions and decision-making about the books (Lee & McCarty, 2017; Nash et al., 2018) (see Figure 3.2).

KNOWINGNESS THROUGH CREATING IDENTITY TEXTS

In the beginning of the year, the teachers engage children in composing "identity texts," or "personal stories written using multiple meaning making modes" (Machado, 2017, p. 318). Composing identity texts "encourages children to use all of their linguistic and semiotic resources in composition" (Machado, 2017, p. 318).

Identity texts that center multilingualism and biliteracy are the beating heart of literacy practices in Alicia's classroom. As a bilingual and dual-language teacher, centering students' linguistic abilities is the centerpiece of her teaching practice. Beyond foregrounding Spanish and English, she nurtures biliteracy through meshing and mixing formal languages and language varieties, or regional linguistic practices (Boutte & Johnson, 2013). For example, one year, she asked children to write across languages and language varieties on cutout speech bubbles; one reads "Porque soy bilingue, puedo bailar and dance" (see Figure 3.3).

La Historia de mi Nombre/The Story of My Name

Another "identity text" Alicia's class engages in creating is la historia de mi nombre (the story of my name). It's adapted from a practice developed by Susi Long (personal communication, 2017, August 7) to "put the importance of children's names front and center in the classroom." First, Alicia reads children's literature that centers on the importance of names (see Figure 3.4).

She then asks students to interview family members about their name's history, with the questions:

- Who named your child?
- Is your child named after someone?
- What is something special about your child's name?

Figure 3.3. "Porque Soy Bilingue"/"Because I'm Bilingual"

Next, children create a "name web" based on their interviews. Finally, children write the stories of their names. A part of one child's finished name story reads: "My name is special because my mom named me. She liked the name Arturo. . . . No one in my family has my name. Not even my tios or abuelo" (as cited in Nash et al., 2018).

Family collages are another form of identity text (pictured in Figure 2.3). Kerry makes family collages by arranging photos of each child and the child's family on a large piece of blue paper, which is then laminated. After children share their collages, she hangs them up so that children have a sense that their families are always present. She also creates two family collage books for the classroom library. Additionally, Kerry creates books that have a photo of each child and a sentence, "My name is [child's name]." These books help children get to know their classmates' names and feel like they are a member of a group—because their photo is in the book! Kerry has also made books that have the first drawing that each child made in kindergarten. When children have opportunities to read self-selected books together, they always seem to gravitate toward these class identity texts, especially early in the year.

Figure 3.4. Children's Books That Center on the Importance of Names

Your Name Is a Song by Jamilah Thompkins-Bigelow

Alma and How She Got Her Name by Juana Martinez-Neal

When Jo Louis Won the Title by Belinda Rochelle and Larry A. Johnson

I Am René, the Boy/Yo Soy René, el Niño by René Colato Laínez

René Has Two Last Names/René Tiene Dos Apellidos by René Colato Laínez

Always Anjali by Sheetal Sheth

My Name Is Yoon by Helen Recorvitz

One way that Roderick has involved children in creating identity texts is through reading *I Am Enough* by Grace Byers. He then invites children to create multimodal texts that reflect the ways in which they are enough. Multimodal texts "blend languages, language varieties, images, and sound that reflect the hybrid ways that students make sense of the world" (Machado, 2017, p. 318). One student used a cardboard pizza box, paper, pom-poms, drawing, and words to draw and label himself. Growing up with an older brother who was an athlete, the student used pom-poms to create his muscles, adding the labels "muscle" and "strong" (see Figure 3.5).

Another identity text that Roderick's class creates at the beginning of the year are "Who Am I" webs. In each "Who Am I" web, children identify their ethnicities, races, languages, interests, and traditions. Roderick then displays the completed webs on a bulletin board. Figure 3.6 provides more detail about how the teachers implement these identity texts.

Figure 3.5. *I Am Enough* **Multimodal Text**

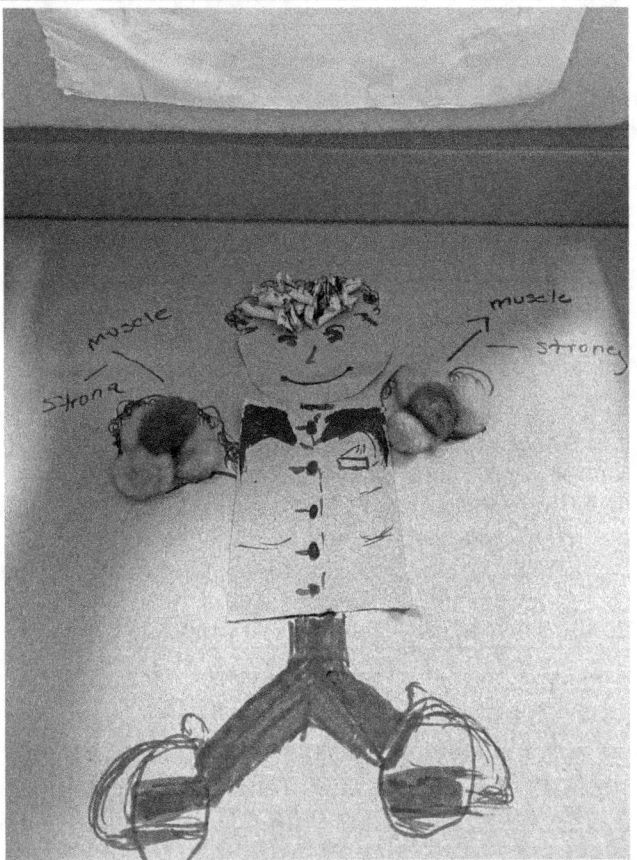

Figure 3.6. Identity Texts in Three Classrooms

Porque Soy Bilingue/Because I'm Bilingual—After reading the poem, "Me x 2/ Yo x 2" by Jane Medina, students respond to the phrases "Porque soy bilingue"/"Because I'm bilingual" (phrases can and should be expanded to include multiple languages spoken within the class) across languages and language varieties on a large speech bubble that is then displayed in the classroom or as a class book.

La Historia de Mi Nombre/Name Stories—Students read about and discuss the importance of names, interview their families, and then write the stories of their names. These name stories can be bound into a class book or displayed on a bulletin board.

Family Collages—Students and teachers gather family photos, paste them on a large blue piece of paper, and laminate them. These can be bound in a class book and hung on a bulletin board with clips so that children can take their family collages down when they feel they need to be close to their families.

My Name Is . . . Class Book—Students and teacher each write a page of this class book by writing or completing the sentence "My name is ____." The teacher places a photo of each child on their page and makes the pages into a class book.

First Day of School Drawing Class Book—Teacher collects the first drawing students make in school. The teacher binds the drawings to make a Class Book.

***I Am Enough* Multimodal Texts**—After reading the book *I Am Enough,* students represent the ways they feel they are enough by creating a multimodal text.

Who I Am Webs—Placing a photo of themselves in the center of a web diagram, children and teachers list their languages, ethnicities, race(s), and cultural heritage(s) to make an "identity web."

CREATING CRITICAL SPACES THROUGH READ-ALOUDS

Reading aloud is a powerful literacy practice that allows teachers to create a culturally sustaining and community-centered classroom climate. Wynter-Hoyte et al. (2019) discuss how read-alouds are culturally sustaining in that they create "critical spaces [that allow] young children and practitioners to engage in discursive situations and practices within their lives" (p. 434).

Illustrating this idea, Roderick often asks families to come into the classroom at the beginning of the year to share their careers, hobbies, cultures, and adventures through a read-aloud. Before the visit, they identify a book that could be shared during their visit. After a family member shares a read-aloud, children have the opportunity to ask questions. This practice helps create a sense of family and community in the classroom. When other children in the class see that family member on other occasions, such as during dismissal, Roderick has observed them saying "hi" as though they are now part of the family. These types of experiences have led Roderick to build longstanding connections years after children have moved on to a new grade or new school.

Kerry also reads books aloud in the beginning of the year to celebrate a diversity of the love, comfort, and communion within homes and families of children, including *Love* by Matt de la Peña and *Saturday* by Oge Mora, which share stories of children interacting with their families at home. Alicia uses many different books to discuss identity, family, and community at the start of the school year. Some include *The Day You Begin* by Jacqueline Woodson and *¡Sí! Somos Latinos/Yes! We are Latinos* by Alma Flor Ada and F. Isabel Campoy. *The Day You Begin* by Jacqueline Woodson is a touchstone text that discusses how to be yourself and be self-confident even in a new classroom of people who "don't quite look like you." One year, Alicia collaborated with Erik Sumner, the art teacher at Northern Parkway and creator of this book's cover art, and read aloud *Black Is a Rainbow Color* by Angela Joy, a book that celebrates the beauty of Blackness in a world that often depicts the color as bad and ugly. Erik created a rainbow mirroring the one depicted in the book on the bulletin board just outside Alicia's classroom. Children then selected photographs, pictures, and illustrations of black and brown items, people, and places to add to the rainbow. As children brought in images of black and brown in their lives, they had many critical insights about the colors black and brown, and all the beautiful things in their lives that were black and brown. For example, a student who had selected images of a brown football, a black car, and a woman with brown skin exclaimed "I didn't realize that some of my favorite things in the world are black and brown!"(see Figure 3.7).

Figure 3.7. Black and Brown Are Rainbow Colors

KNOWINGNESS THROUGH LETTER, SOUND, AND WORD WORK

As they integrate and introduce letter, sound, and word work activities in the beginning of the year, Alicia, Roderick, and Kerry are sensitive to several issues. First, they are attentive to the way Dominant English (DE), a linguistic variety that values midwestern, middle-class, and White American language (Baker-Bell, 2020), is privileged in schools and society. This devaluing of anything other than DE echoes loudly in discourses about language or word gaps. These deficit approaches reify assertions about a *culture of poverty*; framing "the languages and cultures of poor students of color as needing to be fixed and replaced with 'better' languages communicative modes in writing and cultures" (Alim & Paris, 2015, p. 79). Second, the teachers have a depth of knowledge about the complexity of the English language. Finally, they take into consideration the ineffectiveness of bottom-up processing with some of their students, even as they each implement scripted phonics programs.

Dominant English

Jamila Lyiscott's (2014) spoken-word performance *3 Ways to Speak English* poetically highlights her own experience with DE: "I know that I had to borrow your language because mines was stolen/But you can't expect me to speak your history wholly while mines is broken." Lyiscott draws on African American Language (AAL) to underscore the myth of "standard" English and to share the interconnected history of her language, identity, culture, and community (Lippi-Green, 2012; Rosa, 2019; Smitherman, 2006).

Complexity of English

Lyiscott's (2014) truths are echoed by language scholars, who emphasize that language is a complex, fluid, sociocultural practice rather than merely a system of letters, phonemes, and morphological units (García, 2009; Hoffman et al., 2016). Gutiérrez and Rogoff (2003) help represent language as a sociocultural phenomenon with the concept of "repertoires of practice," or "ways of engaging in activities stemming from observing and otherwise participating in cultural practices" (p. 22).

The way that English has shifted over time is a prime example of language's sociocultural and fluid nature. Throughout the ages, English has absorbed many grammatical features of other languages (e.g., German, Norman-French, and Latin-Greek), yet it has maintained the same spelling rules (Share, 2008). As a result, the English writing system (or orthography) is opaque or deep. There are 26 letters (graphemes) and 42 to 44 speech sounds (phonemes), with about 20 vowel phonemes, 6 vowels, and no native diacritic symbols (like the é in soufflé) (Share, 2008). Thus, it can take children 3 years to learn to read in English, as compared to 1 year for languages with a more transparent orthography like Arabic, Italian, or Hebrew (Seymour et al., 2003).

For Alicia, Roderick, and Kerry, teaching children letters, sounds, and words is complex because language is complex. For this reason, while they work to help children learn the alphabetic principle—that there are relationships between letters and sounds (International Literacy Association [ILA], 2019, 2020)—they also honor children's multilingualism and the multiple letters and sounds they know. They do so through encouraging code-meshing, or the use of multiple language varieties, languages, symbols, and communicative modes in writing and speaking (Zapata & Laman, 2016). Another way of honoring the complexity of language is through promoting translanguaging, defined as "the complex [mixing of] languaging practices" (García, 2009, p. 45). The "Porque soy bilingue" speech bubbles illustrate translanguaging and code-meshing as children write across both language varieties and languages (see Figure 3.3).

Phonological and Phonemic Awareness

With the complexity of language in mind, the teachers engage children in developing phonological awareness, or becoming attuned to the phonological units of words. They also help build children's phonemic awareness, which involves isolating, categorizing, and blending phonemes, onsets, and rimes to form words (ILA, 2020). Foundational to culturally sustaining instruction that builds phonological and phonemic awareness is the practice of contrastive analysis, or the explicit juxtaposition of multiple languages and their features by examining similarities and differences (Machado, 2017). For example, to facilitate children's creation of their bilingual speech bubbles (see Figure 3.3), Alicia read aloud the poem "Me x 2/Yo x 2" by Jane Medina, in Spanish and English, and they talked about syllable, word, and sentence differences between the two languages. The poem, from Lee Bennett Hopkins's (2015) children's poetry anthology *Amazing Faces,* starts: "I read times 2/I write times 2/I think, I dream, I cry x 2." It is a foundational text for Alicia as she approaches all literacy instruction, framing the value of multilingualism in her classroom.

Alphabet and Word Walls

The alphabet and word walls in each classroom serve as a visual anchor to connect the written alphabet(s) spoken by the children in their classes to speech sounds. This is important, as letters and sounds should be taught and reviewed simultaneously (Jones & Reutzel, 2012). In each class, children also have a smaller version of the alphabet wall and a list of high-frequency words in their writing notebooks.

As a kindergarten teacher, Kerry spends time each day explicitly teaching children how to write letters. She does this because research shows that teaching just one letter each week doesn't allow enough time for practice (Jones & Reutzel, 2012). For Roderick and Alicia, the alphabet wall is a reinforcement. In Alicia's classroom, the word wall creates an everyday space for contrastive analysis, as children compare Spanish and English high-frequency and vocabulary words on the wall. Roderick's Graffiti Wall holds new and exciting vocabulary words that reflect students' languages, cultures, and interests (more on this in Chapter 5!).

High-Frequency Words

High-frequency words are the words that occur most often in the English language. These words may be irregular words that cannot easily be sounded out. In early childhood, many rely on Fry's (1980) compilation of 300 words to identify high-frequency words, but the teachers also explicitly teach words that reflect children's interests. Kerry and the children look for these high-frequency words in the morning message. Roderick and Alicia give children a personal dictionary with high-frequency words and spaces to write their own words that they can use anytime.

Scripted Phonics Curricula

Roderick and Kerry have a scripted phonics curriculum that their schools require them to use. Despite their scripted curricula, the teachers are careful to not codify their phonics instruction into generic analyses of decontextualized structural linguistic units (Hoffman et al., 2021). This is because they feel (and research confirms) that all learners do not benefit from phonics instruction (Carbo, 1987; Ehri et al., 2001; Noguerón-Liu, 2020; Willis, 2015). For instance, the National Reading Panel report indicates that synthetic, embedded, and systematic phonics, "did not benefit low achieving [LA] poor readers. The overall effect size was close to zero" (Ehri et al., 2001, p. 429; National Reading Panel, 2000).

An example of how Roderick mediates the scripted phonics curriculum at his school is the way he introduces phonics instruction during the first week. He starts the year off by engaging children in real conversations—about anything. He then asks children to really listen to the words they say and the ways people in the classroom talk, prompting them with questions like: "How do we sound?" and "Do we sound like we're from Jamaica? New York? And where in New York—from Long Island? Brooklyn?" and "How do we know that?" He then prompts them to represent some words they noticed by saying the sounds—he asks them to say the first and last sounds and then the middle sound. He does this auditory discrimination activity because he wants children to understand that words are sounds squeezed together to make a word but that language varieties may influence the way children hear and say sounds. Sometimes, if children struggle to discriminate the sounds in auditory discrimination activities like this, the teachers will ask children to close their eyes and participate in a game in which the teacher plays different common sounds from the children's lives—a city bus, a helicopter, water dripping, a door closing, a storm—and children identify the sound they hear (and in their multiple languages, if that's the case).

Bottom-Up Processing

Hollins (2015a) argues that part of the reason that many common approaches to phonics instruction are not effective is because they rely on *bottom-up* processing. Bottom-up processing is influenced by Western, low-context linear and sequential cultural practices. High-context cultures make meaning through *top-down* processing contextualized within the environment. The example of the way Roderick grounded the teaching of letters and auditory discrimination of sounds within children's languages and language varieties showcases a top-down processing approach. By honoring the pluralistic language varieties during phonics instruction, Roderick pushes against notions of Dominant English as a good and right norm. This, and the other practices featured in this chapter, showcase how practices and processes can be contextualized and mediated for particular children, as our models illustrate (see Model and Framework in Figures 1.3 and 1.4).

BEGINNING THE READING AND WRITING WORKSHOP

At the beginning of the year, the teachers establish practices that will guide reading and writing all year. The teachers want to foster reading and writing that help children flexibly and naturally use their languages and cultural ways of being to "make their voices visible" (Dyson, 2013, p. 19). As such, the teachers mediate and hybridize the reading and workshop. *Hybridizing* involves creating spaces and routines where reading and writing processes and practices can be situated within children's cultures. Hybridized spaces are those where children blend, and interweave diverse lifeways of their language, social, and media experiences through literacy acts (Dyson, 2013). This model typically involves the steps shown in Figure 3.8.

The workshop model fosters a "gradual release of responsibility," where teachers apprentice children in learning cycles through modeling and demonstrating complex tasks and procedures, followed by guided and later

Figure 3.8. Structure of Hybridized Reading/Writing Workshop

Mini-lesson: A 5–10-minute lesson to teach content that is culturally sustaining.
Writing/Reading/Conferring: A 15–45-minute block of time where children work on writing and reading in their own languages and about their own heritage and identity. Teachers work with small groups and/or confer with children.
Share time: 5–10 minutes at the end of the block.
Teacher selects or children volunteer to share what they have learned (keeping track of who has shared!)

independent, practice (Rogoff, 2003). The concept of the gradual release of responsibility extends from Vygotsky's idea that "what a child can do with assistance today she will be able to do by herself tomorrow" (1978, p. 87).

Writing Workshop Routines

At the beginning of the year, Roderick approaches writing like a holistic doctor. He wants to understand what the children already know and what they need to work on. For example, on the first day of writing workshop, he often asks children to write down three things they would like him to know about them. Through observing what children write, he is able to build writing routines that support them.

Thinking Notebook. One of the first workshop routines Roderick establishes is the thinking notebook (McCarthy, 2020). In this notebook, children write down their cares, concerns, and connections (see Figure 3.9) to the

Figure 3.9. Thinking Notebook Entry

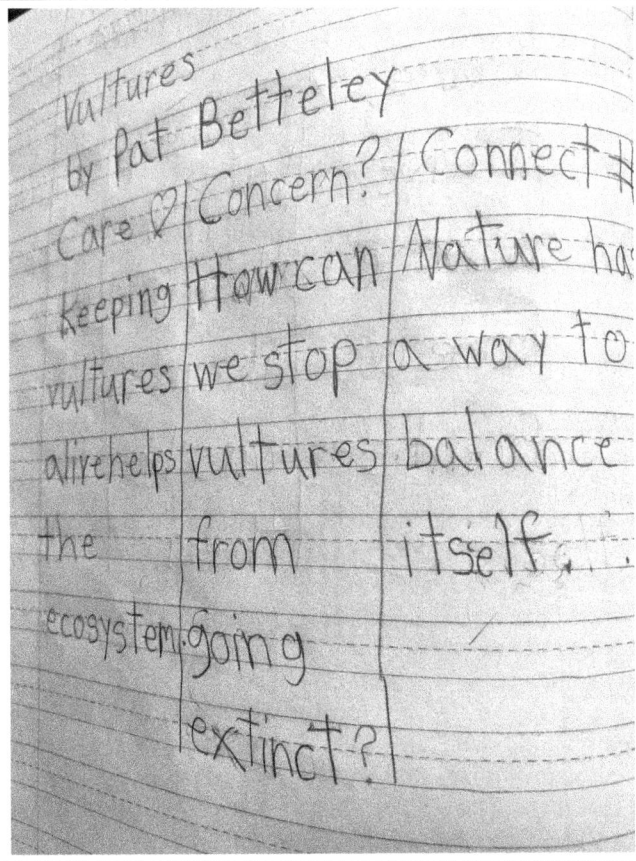

book they are currently reading. By the second week of school, Roderick's class practices this routine of responding to texts in their thinking notebooks every day. As noted above, students sometimes share their thinking notebook entries during morning meeting.

Developing Writerly Selves. Regardless of the grade that Alicia is teaching, she starts writing workshop with the express intention of helping children develop writerly selves. They talk about different writing tools and environmental factors that they each may need to be their best writing selves. They may decorate their writing notebooks. They discuss that some people are easily distracted and may need to choose a spot by themselves or by the windows for better light. All of these different scenarios are discussed, and children decide what would be the best writing spot for them. As they write identity texts about their bilingualism, their names, and their families, they develop confidence in themselves as writers in the classroom space and beyond. This focus on developing writerly selves fosters relationships among the students and helps build Alicia's relationships with them, too. Since the focus is children's development of writerly selves, in the beginning of the year Alicia does not correct children's writing.

Each teacher leads the classroom to practice the writing workshop routines—mini-lesson, independent writing, and share time—each day. Kerry talks with children about the general structure of the workshop: they'll start with a lesson on the rug, then they'll go off to write, then they'll come back together on the rug to share someone's work and see what they can learn from that work. They talk about ways to be independent at writing time and what kind of noise level is helpful. They talk about what "library" voices sound like. They talk about tools writers use, too. Children can use anything from a black flair pen to a pencil—they can choose. Giving children different kinds of choices is one way to help children feel engaged in the writing process and also fosters agency and critical thinking (Hertz & Mraz, 2018).

Making Books. Children in Kerry's class start writing workshop by making books. Kerry thinks that if she asks kids to make books right away, they feel like authors, because they are very familiar with books as a form of writing. They know that books have words and pictures on the pages and that there is a story or series of pieces of information that are presented across the pages. In inviting children to make books, Kerry has been inspired by Glover (2009), Ray and Glover (2008), and Cleaveland (2016). As they begin to make their first books, Kerry and the children often talk about drawing with detail and the setting. Kerry sometimes gives a mini-lesson about how to draw—for example, how to draw a person using ovals. Inviting drawing in the early days of writing is key, as Genishi and Dyson (2009) say, because "drawing in particular is a primary way that many young children, from varied cultures, represent, imagine, and extend their experiences" (p. 25). The way Kerry introduces book-making varies. One year, she started by giving children plain pieces of paper for drawing and then waited to see if kids would start making books out of the paper. After one week, one child folded her paper longways to make a book. Kerry then shared that first book with the rest of the class and invited other students to make the same kind of book. Sometimes she gives children three plain sheets of paper stapled together to make a book. At the beginning of book-making, sometimes Kerry feels worried because the books don't always seem totally complete. But then she remembers that when children make these first books, they are demonstrating that they know a lot already—a squiggly line represents something important in a story. They write words and draw pictures on most of the pages. After the first few weeks of experimenting with making books during writing workshop, Kerry asks children to choose one book that they feel really proud of and add a cover. She will ask children to share their books during the writing share and then place children's books in the classroom library.

Mentor Authors and Illustrators. Writing workshop is connected to reading workshop. Often when Kerry talks about book-making with kids, she showcases the mentor author-illustrators they are reading in reading workshop (Cleaveland, 2016). Many of Kerry's students are Black and Latinx, so she chooses Black and Latinx author-illustrators like Donald Crews, Kadir Nelson, and Monica Brown. Kids get inspired by their books; one of her students really liked *Please, Puppy, Please*, illustrated by Nelson and tried making a book called "Please, Cat, Please."

Reading Workshop

Reading Workshop has the same structure as writing workshop: mini-lesson (with a critical read-aloud), independent reading/small groups, and share time (see Figure 3.9). For Alicia, reading workshop begins by working with children to understand how to select a "perfect fit" book to read independently by reviewing what a "perfect fit" book looks, feels, and sounds like. For example, Alicia teaches children that they know a book is a perfect fit when they feel really interested in the book and can read most of the words. However, Alicia never tells children that they cannot read a certain book. She also works with children to choose a special reading spot. Alicia finds *Charlotte and the Quiet Place* by Deborah Sosin and *How to Read a Book* by Kwame Alexander helpful, as these books allow children to visualize what independent reading time looks, feels, and sounds like.

In Kerry's classroom, there are two kinds of reading times: there's reading during "reading workshop," where children read independently and practice a particular reading skill while Kerry works with children one on one and in small groups; and there's "books on the rug time," in which children read all kinds of books on their own or with a partner and tell themselves the story by "reading the pictures" (Sulzby & Teale, 1991). In the beginning of kindergarten, reading workshop lasts only about 5 minutes. Gradually, the amount of independent reading time increases. In all of the classrooms, reading and writing workshop is hybridized and mixed based on the needs of children. Further, reading and writing units are interconnected. For example, if children are working on writing personal narratives in writing workshop, then they are reading and studying personal narratives during reading workshop (much more on this in later chapters).

CONCLUSION

For many Children of Color, the beginning of school marks a "dramatic departure from the experiential and culturally relevant learning . . . in their community contexts" (Spencer et al., 2011). This fact was illustrated in the opening story about how aggressively two White children in Kerry's class reacted to images of a Black boy's confidence and joy in the book *I Am Every Good Thing*. Culturally sustaining pedagogies require teachers to call out "whiteness (including white normativity, white racism and ideologies of white supremacy) as the problem" (Paris, 2021, p. 368), as Kerry did. Simultaneously, culturally sustaining pedagogies (CSPs) require recentering children as full—as members of communities with essential and valuable ways of being, doing, and knowing.

This is why fostering a sense of knowing and being known through beginning-of-the-year literacy practices that create and sustain the lifeways of communities is vital. By using CSPs in routines like morning meeting; labeling the classroom and library; teaching letters, sounds, and words; and setting up for a hybridized reading and writing workshop, the teachers contend with "how [they] see, listen to, interact with, and respond to students—in humanizing and loving ways" (Kinloch, 2017, p. 39). In that way, children's languages, identities, and literacies *are every good thing*.

CHAPTER 4

"¿Que Piensas?"/"What Do You Think?"
Culturally Sustaining Ways of Reading

Kindel Turner Nash, Alicia Arce-Boardman, Roderick Peele, and Kerry Elson

At the guided reading table with Alicia, five children whisper read ¡*El Fútbol Es Un Golazo!*, a Spanish/English book chosen especially because of the children's keen interest in Argentinian soccer player Lionel Messi. Meanwhile, six girls engage in literature discussion on the rug, reading *Sofia Martinez: Abuela's Birthday* by Jacqueline Jules. The girls adore this text, Alicia says, because they feel Sofia and her Abuela are like them—they speak Spanish and are Latina. Alicia meshes English and Spanish as she questions students: "¿Cómo suena diferente la palabra 'net' en español salvadoreño y hondureño?"/"How does the word 'net' sound different in Salvadoran and Honduran Spanish?" "¿Que piensas?"/"What do you think?"

Culturally sustaining pedagogies (CSPs) can reframe language and literacy teaching, positioning children's languages as strengths rather than deficits (Rosa & Flores, 2017). In the vignette above, Alicia *mediated* guided reading instruction for her Latinx students (Nash et al., 2022). Understanding that children thrive when their languages, identities, and cultures are in the foreground, Alicia and the other teachers create reading processes and practices that are life-affirming and build on their capacities, interests, and values. In this way, they have moved away from reading instruction that positions students as "passive recipient[s] of the text's ultimate meaning" (Stone, 2017, p. 2). This chapter focuses on CSPs that nurture young children's *reading*

Focus Questions: What does current research say about how children learn to read? How might children's ways of knowing, being, and doing be nurtured and extended through reading practices?

growth. Illustrations are rooted in definitions and frameworks described in Chapter 1, and a model describing ways of knowing, being, and reading.

HOW DO CHILDREN LEARN TO READ?

Major shifts in understanding of reading and literacy have occurred since the 1970s. The latest research on reading and literacy strongly support the idea that literacy pedagogies need to build on and sustain *children's fullness*. In building an understanding of CSPs that nurture reading growth, it's important to understand that research and the ways of thinking that have informed it.

Simple, Rope, and Stage Models of Reading

Some widely known models represent reading as a simple and linear series of discrete skills (e.g., simple view of reading) (Gough & Tunmer, 1986). Stage models of reading are also prevalent; these propose that children progress through stages as they learn to read (Chall, 1983; Ehri, 1991; Frith, 1985; Gough et al., 1992). Stage models are rooted in the idea that becoming literate is an emergent process influenced by home and school environments (Morrow et al., 2002). In general, stage models portray reading as progressing through pre-alphabetic, partial alphabetic, and full alphabetic to the consolidated alphabetic stage as children move from basic letter, sound, and print knowledge to the ability to fully decode words (Ehri, 1991). Alicia, Roderick, and Kerry encounter these widely known models in professional development, core reading programs, curricula, and websites.

These models may unwittingly fail to recognize the active, central, situated role of *the reader* in the reading process (Duke & Cartwright, 2021; Street & Street, 1984; Willis, 2015). Further, these models may advance ideas about a "normally developing child" who "lives in a family which should support the child's development through the provision of particular resources and literacy practices" (Larson & Marsh, 2015, p. 4). In order to enact pedagogies that are culturally sustaining, teachers need models of how children learn to read that allow them to divest themselves from "the ways whiteness castes White normed practices and bodies as superior" (Paris, 2021, p. 368).

Context-Based, Complex Reading Models

Context-based, complex models view reading as a situated, meaning-making process and implicate teachers, family and community members, and peers as essential to supporting children in learning to read (Pearson & Hiebert, 2015). Research by Clay (2013) and by Goodman et al. (1987) suggests that children use three cueing systems as they read: meaning (semantics), language structure (syntax), and visual (graphophonics). While reading, they integrate increasingly complex semantic, syntactic, and graphophonic information

(Briceño & Klein, 2019). Similarly, Freebody and Luke's (1990) four-resources model suggests that as children read they take on four roles: (1) code breaker, (2) meaning maker, (3) text user, and (4) text critic.

Humanizing, Culturally Sustaining Model of Reading

In our humanizing, culturally sustaining model, learning to read is also viewed as a complex, situated, meaning-making activity. However, we also see reading as shaped by a readers' culturally and linguistically mediated knowledge (ways of knowing), experiences and relationships (ways of being), and strategic reading processes (ways of reading) (see Figure 4.1). Building on Duke and Cartwright's (2021) active model of reading, which suggests that "readers play a central role in making reading happen" (p. 6), we posit that with children at *the center* of reading, learning to read can be a humanizing and culturally sustaining event that centers children's, families', and communities' cultures and lifeways.

Ways of Knowing. As a reader transacts with a text, they construct meaning based on their cultural and linguistic knowledge. Cultural knowledge "is a group's knowledge production process that occurs as they understand and respond to their reality" (Love, 2019, p. 128). It influences the way children hear and interpret texts (Duke & Cartwright, 2021). For example, when reading *Crown: An Ode to the Fresh Cut* by Derrick Barnes, a book about

Figure 4.1. Ways of Knowing, Being, and Reading

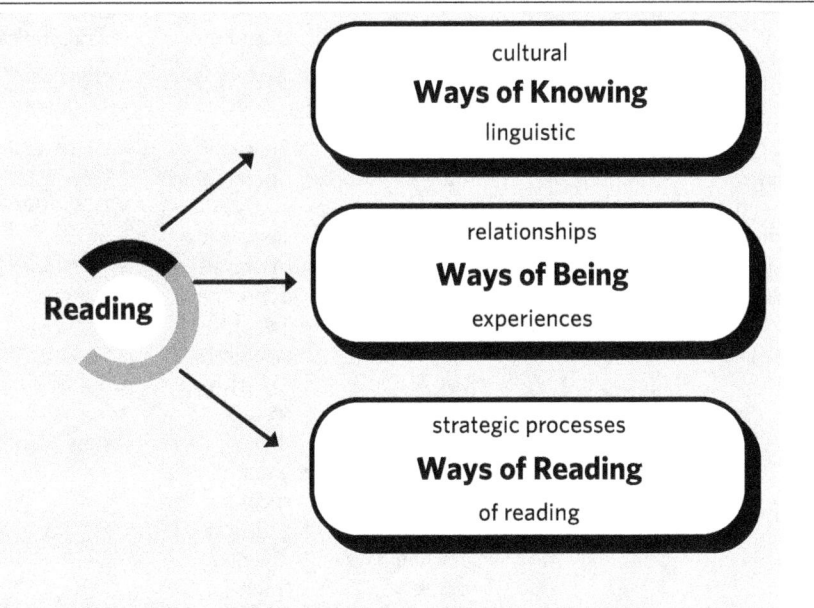

the rich Black community tradition of visiting the barber shop, Kerry noticed that the Black boys in her class listened carefully and looked intently at the pictures.

Alicia, Roderick, and Kerry honor children's linguistic ways of knowing by positioning all human languages and language varieties as structured, patterned, and rule-governed. A language variety is a way of communication linked to a region or social group (Wheeler et al., 2012). For example, Roderick and Alicia speak with a New York English variety because they are from New York, while Kindel has a southern language variety because she is from the southeastern United States.

Raciolinguistics is a concept that focuses on both the "central role that language plays in racialization and on the enduring relevance of race and racism in the lives of People of Color" (Alim, 2016, p. 5). It can help us understand how the languages or language varieties of "certain racialized bodies" are conflated with linguistic deficiency (Rosa & Flores, 2017a, p. 177). For example, although often positioned as substandard or slang by other teachers in Alicia, Roderick, and Kerry's schools, African American Language (AAL) has syntactical, phonological, semantic, and pragmatic rules and features just like Spanish, Amharic, Arabic, Twi, Hebrew, Wolof, Haitian Creole, French, and all other languages (Boutte, 2002; Boutte & Johnson, 2013). Table 4.1 illustrates syntactical, phonological, semantic, and pragmatic features and examples of AAL. However, depending on the global region in the African diaspora where it is spoken, the textures and contours of AAL differ. For

Table 4.1. African American Language and Ways of Knowing

	Syntax Rule-Governed Structure	Phonology Sound/Symbol	Semantics Meaning/Schema	Pragmatics Purposes/Contexts
AAL Features and Examples	• Substitution of -th phoneme (wif, dem, wit) • Different stress patterns (PO-lice) • No distinction between words that sound alike (fine/find) • Consonant blends substituted or deleted (axe/ask)	• Make it simple (You a pretty girl.) • Two or more negatives allowed (You don't have no shoes.) • Use of habitual "be" (She be nice.) • Regularize when possible (We is/She is/They is)	• Frequent use of metaphors and similes/suspension of literal definitions • Tonal semantics ("Girl, you *wearing* that.") • Creativity in speaking • Cultural inversion (phat/fat)	• Call and response • Direct over indirect • Episodic storytelling • Different ways of questioning • Verbal signifying

example, in Jamaican Patois, an AAL variety spoken by many in Roderick's class, children are accustomed to using the greeting "Watagwan?" (meaning What's good? or What's going on?). This greeting contains syntactic, phonological, semantic, and pragmatic features connected to West African language beyond the examples in Table 4.1. In fact, language is so fluid, that youth of different cultural and linguistic backgrounds who are in school together frequently sample and mesh each other's languages (Paris, 2009).

Ways of Being. Ways of being are often unseen belief systems that guide human behavior and values (Hollins, 2019). Life experiences, relationships, and cultural community membership shape ways of being (Gutiérrez & Rogoff, 2003). People have different ways of being because they have different ways of thinking grounded in their ancestral knowledge, experiences, and relationships as members of communities. Some groups of people think in analytic ways, others in more holistic ways (Yama & Zakaria, 2019). Analytic thinking is distinguished by the use of logic, visual attention, and taxonomic categorization by rules. Holistic thinking, on the other hand, is characterized by family orientation and thematic categorization by relationships and an emphasis on context and situational logic (Hollins, 2019; Kelkar et al., 2013). Ways of being naturally impact the ways people transact with texts (Baker-Bell, 2020; Gee, 1999; Rosenblatt, 1994; Smagorinsky, 2001; Street & Street, 1984). For example, Alicia has found that the multilingual, Latinx and Afro-Latinx children in her classes benefit from holistic interactions—such as talking, speaking, listening, and writing together about ideas and texts—rather than from analytic interactions such as completing a sequencing worksheet.

Ways of Reading. Ways of reading include three strategic reading processes (see Figure 4.2). Each of these strategic processes overlaps with a child's ways of knowing and being. Strategic processes build self-regulation, or the

Figure 4.2. Strategic Processes of Reading

Culturally Mediated Cognition
Includes culturally mediated cognitive processes such as working memory, planning, attentional control, self-regulation, and other skills needed to perform complex tasks such as reading.

Motivation to Read
Refers to students' interest in reading and whether they think reading has value; can also refer to students' mindsets around reading success and difficulty.

Reading Strategies
Refers to ways readers approach text to decode and understand it, such as breaking a word into chunks to decode it or using context clues to figure out a word. Interconnected reading strategies focus on decoding, comprehension, fluency, and vocabulary.

means to actively coordinate and solve problems that arise during reading (Duke, 2020). Children's sociocultural context culturally mediates their ways of reading.

Culturally Mediated Cognition. Cognitive processes develop in the context of ancestral knowledge and values (Hollins, 2019). Ancestral knowledge "embodies the developmental progression and collective knowledge of a particular cultural group" (Hollins, 2019, p. 46). Hollins (2015a) describes culturally mediated cognition as the way memory and intellect are generated and strengthened within cultural contexts. Similarly, executive functioning is critical to learning to read (Duke & Cartwright, 2021; Shanahan, 2020a). *Executive function* refers to the cognitive functions that guide attentional control, working memory, and metalinguistic awareness (Adesope et al., 2010; Bialystok, 2011). Executive functioning is linked to cultural and linguistic contexts. For example, Western cultures use rule-based logic and analytical thinking strategies, while Eastern cultures prioritize holistic and perceptual relationships to solve complex cognitive tasks (Kelkar et al., 2013). Further, studies of multilingualism's impact on cognitive functioning show that it leads to increased executive function (Bialystok, 2011; Doucet, 2017). In humanizing, culturally sustaining reading processes, executive function can be leveraged by connecting ancestral knowledge to the reading process.

For instance, Zentella (2015) discusses how in her own Puerto Rican and Mexican household, book reading was not valued. Although her family didn't read books at home, literacy practices such as playing Scrabble with English words, reading the Spanish names on all the picture cards in weekly games of Lotería, reciting Spanish prayers and songs at home and in church, or reciting Spanish poems at cultural soireés took center stage in daily life. Although her teachers did not try to understand her families' literacy practices, if they had done so, as Alicia, Roderick, and Kerry strive to do, they would have been culturally mediating the executive functioning processes Zentella learned and practiced at home.

Culturally mediated cognition goes beyond the popular concepts of learning styles, multiple intelligences, and cultural characteristics. These approaches suggest that teachers organize their lessons around auditory, kinesthetic, visual methods or static aspects of cultural groups (Gardner & Hatch, 1989). Alicia, Roderick, and Kerry do not organize their reading instruction using those static concepts. Instead, they employ pedagogies that sustain culture and go beyond such surface-level approaches. They use practices from children's homes and communities and mediate epistemic and schoolwide reading practices to "work toward reclamation of the histories, contribution, and possibilities of cultural communities" (Gutiérrez & Johnson, 2017, p. 249). One example from Alicia's classroom involved a study of Salsa (Cuban and Puerto Rican) and Mambo (Cuban) music and dancing through an extended exploration of the lives and history of the Afro-Latinx artists, Celia Cruz and Tito Puente. Brought about by a child (Latinx, from El Salvador) who made a comment about the skin of another child (Latinx, from Dominican Republic) being too dark, Alicia wanted to engage in a pro-Black study of Afro-Latinx artists to expand children's thinking about connections between African and Latinx people. Children read multiple books, such as *My Name Is Celia/ Me Llamo Celia: The Life of Celia Cruz* and *Tito Puente, Mambo King/Tito Puente: Rey del Mambo* by Monica Brown, interviewed family members who loved these forms of dancing, watched original videos of Puente and Cruz performing, practiced dancing, and wrote detailed responses to those texts.

The teachers are able to foster culturally mediated cognition by forming deep connections to children's cultural communities via cultural membership or apprenticeship (Hollins, 2015a). This is why, as previous chapters showcased, Alicia, Roderick, and Kerry spend time in the homes and the communities of the children they teach each year! How could they sustain and culturally mediate children's ways of knowing and being if they didn't truly know the children?

Motivation to Read. If children's languages, cultures, and interests are centered in the reading process, they will be more motivated to read. The example of Kerry's Black students sitting up and paying close attention to the book *Crown: Ode to the Fresh Cut* illustrates this. If motivated to read, children in turn develop self-extending reading behaviors such as using reading strategies to figure out tricky words (Clay, 2013). Synthesizing reading motivation research with CSPs, there are five key practices that foster reading motivation:

- **Relevance:** Children can connect texts to their own experiences, languages, and cultures.
- **Choice:** Children have choices within the curriculum and classroom.
- **Collaboration:** Children have opportunities to work together.
- **Self-efficacy support:** Children set reasonable goals for their work.
- **High reading volume:** Children read widely, extensively, and for a variety of purposes (Duke & Martin, 2011; Guthrie & Klauda, 2014; Guthrie, 2015).

Reading Strategies. Reading strategies are "deliberate, goal-directed attempts . . . to decode text, understand words, and construct meanings of text" (Afflerbach et al., 2008, p. 365). Reading strategies are mental activities initiated by the child to problem-solve the puzzle of reading (Clay, 2013). Strategies are different from skills, which are strategies that have become automatic (Afflerbach et al., 2008). Delpit (2012) discusses the importance of explicitly teaching strategies in ways that are: "(1) situated within engaging activities; (2) embedded in real writing, reading, and communication or, if taught in isolation, put immediately into context . . . and (3) taught flexibly when needed, rather than as an unvarying curriculum" (pp. 63–64). Table 4.2 shares definitions and examples from the teachers' classrooms of reading strategies for decoding, fluency, comprehension, and vocabulary.

Table 4.2. Reading Strategies for Decoding, Fluency, Comprehension, and Vocabulary

Reading Strategy	Looks Like	Sounds Like
Decoding/Word Identification Breaking the code of written texts through using knowledge of the alphabet, phonemes, spelling, and syntax or language structure to pronounce words	Doing auditory-discrimination activities Connecting graphemes (letters) to sounds (phonemes) by blending and manipulating the sounds to say the word or reading the word from memory	"Listen to the word. What sounds do you hear first/next/last?" "Listen to your classmate's words. What sounds do you hear?" "Look at the word." "Tap out all the sounds you hear." "Try to connect one sound to the next." "Glide through all the sounds." "Think about what makes sense." "Does my idea for the word match what is happening in the book?"
Fluency Bridging accuracy and comprehension by reading with prosody, or expressive oral language	Being attentive to the ways that oral reading makes sense and sounds right, and when it doesn't, rereading to make sure it does	"Use your 'crisp pointer' finger to track the words while reading." "Scoop up the phrases in this sentence so it sounds more like how you sound when you are talking." "Read it again." "Act out what you read."
Comprehension Using, understanding, composing, and critiquing meaningful written, visual, and spoken texts	Figuring out the meaning of smaller and larger parts of texts	"What does that word mean?" "Why are we reading this text?" "What connections do you have to this text?" "How does this text compare and contrast?" "How can you use prior knowledge?" "What do we wonder about while reading?" "What movies play in your mind while reading?"
Vocabulary Going from the printed form of a word to its meaning	Figuring out the meaning of unfamiliar words and sentences based on prior knowledge of the word or sentence and from context clues like illustrations, other resources, or by getting clues from the parts of the word (morpheme)	"Let's look at the parts of the word to figure out its meaning." "Let's talk about some words we will see in this book." (before reading) "What do you think this word means?" (during reading) "This word means xx." (during reading)

By providing ample reading time and culturally sustaining reading practices that build on children's ways of knowing, being, and reading, the children in Alicia, Roderick, and Kerry's classrooms become increasingly engaged in applying the reading strategies they are learning.

CULTURALLY SUSTAINING READING PRACTICES

Alicia, Roderick, and Kerry's teaching elucidates the humanizing, culturally sustaining model of learning to read that we have just described. Every day, the teachers strive to honor and extend children's ways of knowing, being, and reading by engaging in culturally sustaining reading practices. These practices fall within two domains: life-affirming ways of reading and providing time to read and talk about reading.

LIFE-AFFIRMING WAYS OF READING

Alicia, Roderick, and Kerry want their reading instruction to be life-affirming. Bartolomé (1994) argued that "[u]nless educational methods are situated in the students' cultural experiences, students will continue to show difficulty" (p. 191). Life-affirming teaching builds motivation for reading in ways that help children understand themselves and their cultures (Camangian & Cariaga, 2021).

CLASSROOM LIBRARY

Classroom libraries are at the heart of life-affirming reading instruction. As you have read, the teachers' classroom libraries are filled with books that reflect children's interests, languages, and histories. They create what Bishop (1990) calls mirrors, windows, and sliding glass doors for children. Children engage with the classroom library during self-selected independent reading, literature discussion groups, daily interactive read-alouds, and guided reading. Curating a library that contains mirror, window, and sliding glass door texts is a foundational first step in culturally mediated cognition. Yet creating a classroom library that builds from children's ancestral knowledge has its challenges. Since the 1960s, more than 85% of all children's and young adult literature spotlights White characters (Cooperative Children's Book Center, 2019). Another challenge is that books by Black, Latinx, Indigenous, and Other People of Color are hard to access (Thomas, 2016). Figure 4.3. shares trusted resources and children's book awards that the teachers have come to utilize over time to set up life-affirming classroom libraries.

Figure 4.3. Resources for Building a Culturally Sustaining Classroom Library

Resources	Children's Book Awards
American Indians in Children's Literature	Américas Award
The Brown Bookshelf	American Indians in Children's Literature Best Books
Mango and Marigold Press	
Cooperative Children's Book Center	Asian/Pacific American Award for Literature
Kitaab World	
Latinos in Kid Lit	Carter G. Woodson Award
#We Need Diverse Books	Coretta Scott King Award
Social Justice Books	Tomás Rivera Award
South Asians in Children's Lit	Pura Belpré Award
First Book Marketplace	Stonewall Book Awards List
@teachfor the change (Instagram)	
@black_education_matters (Instagram)	

Everyday Talk and Critical Questions

To culturally mediate their reading instruction, the teachers have to understand *how* children think. Thus, children's everyday talk and questions often inspire reading instruction. Everyday talk and critical questioning also help children to build oral and reading comprehension through strategies like making connections to prior knowledge, comparing and contrasting, and asking or responding to questions that spark their critical consciousness. For example, Roderick's 2nd-graders learned about Juneteenth, the oldest national holiday commemorating the end of human enslavement of People of African descent in the United States. He used several different forms of media to explore Juneteenth, including the children's books *Juneteenth: A Children's Story* by Opal Lee and *Juneteenth: A Celebration* by Courtney Juste, a YouTube video called "Juneteenth for Kids!" produced by Seed of Melanin Kids!, and Black History Flashcards (which children explore throughout the year, not just during African American history month). Connecting to ancestral knowledge about Black freedom traditions, one child exclaimed, "Juneteenth reminds me of the Haitian Revolution!" This child's family celebrated Haitian Independence Day on January 1, which marks the date in 1804 when Haiti became the first Black republic and the first Western country to abolish chattel enslavement (Embassy of Haiti, 2021).

Another example occurred one year as a student in Roderick's class proclaimed that he wanted to teach the class "that Rosa Parks was the first Black woman to not give up her seat on the bus." The child had read that misinformation in an article about Rosa Parks from an online news magazine for kids. In fact, Rosa Parks was *not* the first Black woman to protest segregationist laws and policies in the Jim Crow era; it was Claudette Colvin (see learningforjustice.org/magazine/publications/beyond-the-bus). Based on the child's everyday curiosity and desire to share with his classmates, Roderick talked to the class about how Claudette Colvin had refused to give up her bus seat 9 months before Parks did so. In this way, he used this as an opportunity to pose an essential question leading the kids to be critical readers and consumers of texts: "If the books or articles we read do not give us true or accurate information, what should we do?" Then, they explored, through ongoing discussions of books and online videos, the question, "What does it mean to be an activist for justice?" like both Claudette Colvin and Rosa Parks.

Kerry often finds that children's critical questions and reflections can lead to curricula in which children learn more about their own cultures and those of their classmates. For example, one year, some of Kerry's students shared that they liked the song "Happy Birthday" by Stevie Wonder and sang it when they celebrated birthdays. Kerry previously had only sung "Happy Birthday to You" by Patty and Mildred Hill at classroom birthday celebrations; that was the song that her own White family had sung at birthdays. Kerry realized that by singing only the Hill sisters' song in the classroom, she was centering her own cultural background rather than her students'. Kerry then launched a curriculum in which she and her students learned about birthday songs from each other's families; sharing songs in many languages, including Spanish, French, Hebrew, and Japanese (Elson, 2019). They read books about birthdays and birthday traditions and wrote their own class birthday song with phrases from the birthday songs they had shared from home.

Reading and Writing Against Oppression

Offering life-affirming reading instruction that centers children in the reading process means being prepared to respond to what is going on in the world and to how it is constrained by systems of oppression—racism, sexism, linguicism, xenophobia, heterosexism, and ableism. Boutte and Muller (2018) point out "we should be cognizant that young children are very astute at figuring out the socio-political dynamics within schools and society" (p. 2). Since our society is not politically neutral, the teachers feel it is their responsibility to *lean in* to sociopolitical realities and read and write in response to it.

For example, the teachers used interactive read-alouds as a jumping off point to help kids sort through the anti-immigrant and xenophobic discourses and threats of deportation they heard during the Trump presidency. For example, they read books like *When a Bully Is President: Truth and Creativity for Oppressive Times* by Maya Christina Gonzalez, *Separate Is Never Equal: Sylvia Mendez and Her Family's Fight for Desegregation* by Duncan Tonatiuh, and *This Book Is Anti-racist: 20 Lessons on How to Wake Up, Take Action, and Do the Work* by Tiffany Jewell. All these texts highlight specific actions that kids can take to counter oppressive ideas and discourses

Figure 4.4. Teacher Resources for Reading and Writing Against Oppression

Dunn, A. H. (2021). Teaching on days after: Educating for equity in the wake of injustice. Teachers College Press.
https://www.facebook.com/groups/teachingondaysafter/

Learning for Justice (formerly Teaching Tolerance)
https://www.learningforjustice.org/

Teaching for Change: Building Social Justice Starting in the Classroom
https://www.teachingforchange.org/

Abolitionist Teaching Network
https://abolitionistteachingnetwork.org/

Rethinking Schools
https://rethinkingschools.org/

---

that they may hear, such as writing letters to political figures, or expressing anger in creative ways, such as making videos or other texts. Creating space to explore these ideas was important to Alicia in particular, because she had immigrant students whose parents were fearful of deportation. Figure 4.4 offers a selection of resources that have been helpful for building curriculum and instruction in which children read and write against oppression.

Building on the fundamental principle that culturally sustaining literacy pedagogies need to be life-affirming—to help children understand themselves and their own fullness—the next section details further sustaining approaches to teaching reading, focusing on providing ample time for reading and talking.

Time to Read and Time to Talk

Alicia, Roderick, and Kerry know that children learn to read through reading—five decades of reading research shows the correlation between reading proficiency and reading volume (Allington et al., 2015; van Bergen et al., 2020). While teachers, families, and texts are key, *readers* are central to making reading happen (Pearson & Hiebert, 2015). Time spent reading helps kids stay engaged and practice their decoding, fluency, vocabulary, and comprehension strategies. Through reading, children put together the continuous and complex processes necessary to be a reader (Duke & Cartwright, 2021). Reading proficiency has to do with reading volume and reading instruction *at school* (van Bergen et al., 2020). Yet some studies estimate that American children only spend about *7–8 minutes* per day actually practicing reading in school (Allington et al., 2015).

Text complexity is also important. Children need to read texts that are challenging, not just texts that are on their "level" (Shanahan, 2020a). Independent and small-group/guided reading are key practices in Alicia, Roderick, and Kerry's classrooms that help kids learn to read through reading. While the teachers use a reading workshop structure (see Figure 3.9) and plan units of study with other teachers on their grade level based on reading standards, school curricula and scope and sequence charts can also be used, although these will necessarily need to be mediated for the students at hand.

Independent Reading

Independent reading is a protected instructional practice in the teachers' classrooms, not an extra, add-on time. Included in the hybridized reading workshop and at least one other time frame, it is a time for children to practice strategic reading strategies as they learn them. Children not only develop stamina and independence when they read independently (Allington et al., 2015), they also learn to self-regulate or solve problems and do the best they can to figure out words (Duke & Cartwright, 2021).

In Kerry's class, independent reading is a relaxing time. Her kindergarten class starts with just 5 minutes of reading time so that kids can practice the routine and build stamina (the ability to sustain effort without support from adults) (Hiebert, 2015). In general, the number of minutes children can spend independently reading corresponds with their age. If children are interested and connected to the text, then their motivation and ability to focus increases (Taberski, 2017). By the end of kindergarten, Kerry aims for 15 minutes. By the end of 1st grade, she aims for 20 minutes of independent reading during the allotted time.

In Alicia's class, independent reading is also relaxing—for her students, this is fun reading. There are no assignments attached, and books are not assigned—children can self-select texts. As noted in Chapter 3, for Alicia, text selection begins with working with children to choose books that are the "perfect" fit. In Roderick's class, independent reading offers opportunities for kids to explore themselves by self-selecting books that create a sense of joy and curiosity.

Roderick pays close attention to the books children select so that he can engage with them to discuss the book one-on-one during reading conferences. A reading conference is a time to confer with children, to listen to them read, and to provide feedback and guidance on strategies they might use as they continue reading independently (more on this in Chapter 7). Alicia, Roderick, and Kerry try not to take a rigid approach to text selection in independent reading. However, at Kerry's school, kids do receive preassigned bags of leveled books.

While there are online texts that kids can read on their tablets or on the computer, the tactile sensation of flipping pages and having a bodily experience with books emphasizes the value of reading and is a better support for the development of reading proficiency (McGeown et al., 2016). During independent reading, the teachers work with children in small groups.

Small-Group/Guided Reading

Working with children in small groups allows Alicia, Roderick, and Kerry to meet students' needs more precisely and frequently than if they were to teach only to the whole class. The teachers strive to make sure that groups are fluid and heterogeneous. Creating small groups, the teachers plan backward, always keeping in mind: (a) the purpose for teaching the lesson, (b) the type of strategies they will use to assist children in accomplishing the common group goal, (c) how they will make the lesson fun and engaging, (d) what in-the-moment shifts they will make if children do not understand, and (e) how they will challenge children's thinking.

Guided reading is currently the most widely used approach to small-group reading instruction in U.S. schools. It typically takes place during the middle part of the reading workshop, as other children engage in independent reading (see Figure 3.9). This approach is characterized by small, rotating teacher-directed groups, teacher-selected texts, word work, and reading and talking about reading and writing (Fountas & Pinnell, 2017). The guided reading practice of "matching" children to "instructional" level books has been in place for a century (Shanahan, 2020b).

However, Alicia, Roderick, and Kerry take a different approach. They *mediate and adjust* small-group guided reading instruction with three routine practices:

1) dynamically grouping students based on evolving, hybrid identities;
2) intentionally choosing texts that reflect their students' syncretic cultures, languages, and repertoires of practice; and
3) centering languages through translanguaged and code-meshed writing and talking (Nash et al., 2022).

Dynamically Forming Small Groups. Although the practice has been widely criticized, small groups for guided reading are still commonly formed based on a child's "reading level." There are two ways of determining a text's level or "readability." One involves examining its vocabulary and sentence complexity to achieve a text complexity gradient or Lexile level (Stenner, 1996). Another is based on a system developed by Clay (2013) and Pinnell and Fountas (2010), in which experts create levels for texts from A to Z based on vocabulary, text structure, genre, content, themes, and sentence complexity.

Children are then assessed and assigned to a homogeneous small group based on one of three levels: independent, instructional, and frustration. These levels are determined by a running record of oral reading fluency (Clay, 2013). Many argue that children are only supposed to read texts independently at their independent level—books where they can read 95% of the words (Stahl et al., 2019). However, limiting children in 2nd grade and above to books they can already read stymies opportunities to interact with complex language and vocabulary. In 2nd–3rd-grade small groups, children should read high-interest books that are at "frustration" level (Shanahan, 2020b). This is important because, although all children should have access to reading that promotes dynamic, agentive learning, White students typically have these experiences while many students of Color do not (Adair et al., 2017).

Kindergarten and 1st grade may be the only levels at which children should be practicing reading independently with texts that are relatively readable (like those at their independent level) and reading instructional level texts in small groups (Shanahan, 2020a). Alicia, Roderick, and Kerry give running records to determine reading levels (more on this in Chapter 7), but they have flexibility about how they group children based on hybrid and fluid identities. For example, Roderick asks children to set their own goals and creates groups based on those goals. The teachers also create groups based on children's personalities. Roderick and Alicia have included outgoing children in groups with children who are hesitant to talk and interact with others. In line with the research about grouping in kindergarten and 1st grade, Kerry *does* form small groups based on instructional level.

Intentionally Choosing Texts. In classrooms where guided reading is used, teachers and schools typically create leveled book libraries in order to match student groups with appropriate texts (Fountas & Pinell, 2012). Neither Roderick nor Alicia exclusively use instructional leveled texts in small group guided reading. For example, one week Alicia intentionally selected the bilingual text *Abuela* by Arthur Dorros for one of her guided-reading groups, rather than the Spanish version of a leveled text about Babe Ruth that other 3rd-graders in Alicia's school were reading. While Alicia used *Abuela* with her group, a group of seven girls engaged in a lively and completely student-led literature discussion group on the rug about the book *Sofia Martinez: Abuela's Birthday* by Jacqueline Jules.

While the children in her group of six had an instructional level of "D," Alicia felt the level "L" book was more engaging (Level D texts are typical for children in 1st grade, while Level L texts are typical for children in 2nd–3rd grade). Four of the six children in the group read *Abuela* with a partner, taking turns reading and writing and drawing summaries about the characters in Spanish and English on brightly colored sticky notes. At the same time, Alicia read *Abuela*, page by page, aloud to two other students—a boy, Jhovany, was newly arrived from the Dominican Republic, and a girl, Griselda, had recently emigrated with her family from El Salvador. Alicia stopped periodically to ask questions, provoke insights, and elicit connections:

- What is that word?
- Where do you think they are?
- What is happening here?
- What do you think about this picture?

- Where is Abuela?
- Are the characters really flying?

Because of the support and structure she provided to this group, all the children were able to read this difficult text closely, analyze vocabulary in the text, and practice key reading strategies (like decoding words in Spanish and English, summarizing text, identifying vocabulary, and more). This dynamic grouping is critical to Alicia, because she believes her students' identities are hybrid and dynamic, developed across sites of participation and membership (Hall & Cook, 2012; Kirkland & Hull, 2011). Further, the intentional inclusion of bilingual, challenging texts like *Abuela* supports the development of whole identities rather than fractured ones. In other words, as students access that text and others like it, they hear language that develops, grows, and describes their identities and community memberships (Lippi-Green, 2012).

Decodable Texts. To enable children to practice decoding strategies and develop fluency, the teachers also use "decodable texts" in small-group instruction. Based on her 15 years of experience, Kerry thinks that doing kindergarten and 1st-grade guided reading with instructional-level books and decodable texts can be helpful for some children. She finds that these kinds of texts can help kids read books that are interesting and meaningful and help them learn high-frequency words. Kerry tries to find instructional-level books for small group reading that relate to kids' experiences; however, she is often limited to the books that her school owns. Decodable texts are also not always engaging, but there are several good resources that the teachers draw from (see Figure 4.5).

Centering Languages. In multilingual classrooms, oral language development is critical. Centering languages through translanguaging and

Figure 4.5. Decodable Text Resources

Reading A-Z
readinga-z.com

Flyleaf Publishers
flyleafpublishing.com

Express Readers
express-readers.com

Whole Phonics
whole-phonics.com

Beanstalk Books
beanstalkbooks.com

code-meshing during guided reading helps develop literacy across two or more languages (Zapata & Laman, 2016). For example, in the guided-reading group with the book *Abuela*, Alicia encouraged a young boy to look at the pictures as he read: "Miras a los ilustraciones [Look at the illustrations]." She told the child, "Even if you covered up the words you can tell what is happening by looking at the pictures."

Alicia asks questions in English and Spanish, such as in the vignette that opened this chapter, and connects to language variations of Spanish (code-meshing). For example, when reading *¡El Fútbol Es un Golazo!*, she engaged students in thinking about their language varieties as they discussed the word *net* in Salvadoran and Honduran Spanish. These examples model the way Alicia drew on the flexible ways that multilingual children can navigate texts and the world, without compartmentalizing or erasing their linguistic dexterity (Nash et al., 2022). Kerry and Roderick also work to center children's multiple languages through inviting children to use the above strategies. In addition to independent and small-group and guided reading, interactive read-alouds are central.

Interactive Read-Alouds

Interactive read-aloud is a systematic approach in which teachers engage children in the "what" and "how" of reading. Interactive read-alouds are spaces to model fluent and expressive reading, translanguaging, reading strategies, thoughtful questioning, and exploring vocabulary (Biemiller & Boote, 2006; Harvey & Goudvis, 2007; Osorio, 2020; Smolkin & Donovan, 2000). They can lead to gains in vocabulary and comprehension (Duke & Martin, 2011). Alicia, Roderick, and Kerry use read-alouds to explicitly teach comprehension reading strategies, as illustrated in the following examples:

- **Accessing and using prior knowledge**—Before reading *My First Trip to Africa* by 8-year-old Atlantis Tye Browder, Roderick asks children to think about their "first trips."
- **Setting a purpose for reading/prediction**—When Kerry reads aloud, she shows children the front cover and asks them to predict the story based on what they see.
- **Thinking about text structure**—When reading aloud *Njinga of Ndongo and Matamba* by Ekiuwa Aire, Roderick asks students to think about the beginning, middle, and end.
- **Inferencing**—When reading aloud *I Am René, the Boy/Yo Soy René, el Nino* by René Colato Laínez during an exploration about the importance of names, Alicia gives 2nd-grade students sticky notes and asks them "What can we infer about the author?"
- **Asking questions and wondering**—When reading aloud *René Has Two Last Names/René Tiene Dos Apellidos* by René Colato Laínez, Alicia asks "What would you ask the author?"

- **Identifying story elements**—When Kerry reads *Thank you, Omu!* by Oge Mora, she defines the words "character," "setting," and "events" and invites children to identify those elements in the story.
- **Visualization**—When reading aloud *We Are the Water Protectors* by Carole Lindstrom in a study of Indigenous perspectives on relationships with land and water, Roderick asks students to close their eyes and see the movie that is playing in their head, because this is what some good readers do.
- **Summarizing reading to determine importance**—After reading *I Walk with Vanessa: A Picture Book Story About a Simple Act of Kindness* by Kerascoët, Alicia asks children to summarize the important acts of kindness in the book.
- **Critiquing**—After children in Alicia's class engaged in a text set—*We Are Still Here* by Traci Sorrell, *Encounter* by Jane Yolen, and *Indigenous People's Day* by Katrina Phillips—they wrote argumentative paragraphs about whether or not they thought Columbus Day should be changed to Indigenous People's Day.

CONCLUSION

Genishi and Dyson (2009) urge us to "reimagine language standards in the absence of a standard or generic child" (p. 32). Unlike models of reading that undergird linear, formulaic "standard" or "best practices," culturally sustaining, humanizing reading pedagogies can be fluid, dynamic, and life-affirming—honoring ways of knowing, being, and reading already present in communities. In this way, we can reframe learning to read beyond a standard or generic child, placing children at the center of reading, asking, "¿Que piensas?"/"What do you think?"

CHAPTER 5

I Am Enough
Culturally Sustaining Approaches to Oral Language and Vocabulary Development

Kindel Turner Nash, Alicia Arce-Boardman, Roderick Peele, and Kerry Elson

One spring day, Grace Byers reads her book, *I Am Enough* via the Netflix Bookmarks read-aloud series featuring Black authors. After engaging in the book with illustrations by Keturah Bobo, Roderick asks the 2nd-graders to think about the theme, "Life is about doing the best with what you have *because you are enough.*" He asks, "What does 'I am enough' mean?" "How am I enough?" One student responded, "I am enough because my family loves me, no matter what." Others exclaimed, "I'm enough because I know three languages!" and "I am enough because I have big muscles; I am strong." Another student proclaimed, "I'm enough because I know a lot about my family's history!"

This chapter focuses on the ways that Alicia, Roderick, and Kerry help children feel *they are enough* through the ways they cultivate students' oral language and vocabulary. For too long, oral language and vocabulary scholarship has focused on the perceived language gaps or other deficits of children and families who have a low income or do not speak English as their first language (e.g., Hart and Risley's [1995] methodologically flawed word-gap study). Inherently, this kind of scholarship centers around the question: "How can 'we' get 'these' working-class kids of color to speak/write/be more like middle-class White ones?" (Alim & Paris, 2017, p. 3).

Many well-known texts about oral language and vocabulary development start by rehearsing dominant narratives like *They don't talk or read to their children*, or *They have limited language skills and limited vocabulary knowledge.* In contrast, culturally sustaining oral language and vocabulary

---

Focus Question: How can oral language and vocabulary development be facilitated through culturally sustaining pedagogies?

development practices build on and extend the innate fullness and impressive language abilities of children and families.

ALL CHILDREN HAVE IMPRESSIVE LANGUAGE ABILITIES

As they foster oral language and vocabulary development in multilingual classroom contexts, Alicia, Roderick, and Kerry know that all children have "impressive language abilities, large vocabularies, complex grammar, and deep understandings of experiences and stories" (Wynter-Hoyte et al., 2019, p. 437). In addition, they know that children are cultural beings who use language across events, in community, and through multiple channels (Halliday, 1978; Tolentino, 2007). Over the years, they have developed effective practices that foster and sustain the oral language and vocabulary development of the children they teach. These practices involve comparing, hybridizing, and meshing languages and language varieties across linguistic and cultural repertoires (Gort & Pontier, 2013; Gort & Sembiante, 2015; Machado, 2017). They also work to create classrooms that are agentic sites—spaces that foster critical talk and cooperative thinking—of these multilingual talk and play practices. As they mediate practices for oral language and vocabulary development, the teachers consider:

1) In what way does the classroom talk and discourse reflect children's cultures?
2) Do children have the opportunity to share their cultural and linguistic identities?
3) Whose voices are engaged, and whose are silenced? How are relationships created across differences?
4) What modes of communication are privileged in meaning-making?

ORAL LANGUAGE DEVELOPMENT

Oral language is the system of sounds, words, sentences, and utterances through which all humans express knowledge, ideas, and feelings through talk and discourse (Pearson & Hiebert, 2015). Talk, or what Gee (2007) calls "little d/discourse" involves language use in everyday interactions. Talk is enacted within what Gee calls the macro-structure of "big D/Discourse," or culturally rooted ways of being and doing in the world. Other "modes" of communication beyond talk include nonverbal gestures, gazes, and multimodal/digital forms.

Diglossia and heteroglossia inform culturally sustaining approaches to oral language development. Diglossia describes the ways that some language varieties are positioned as prestigious while others are situated as nonprestigious (Fishman, 1967; Rosa & Flores, 2017a). Heteroglossia expresses the simultaneous use of different linguistic forms or signs and the sociohistorical tensions therein (Martin-Jones et al., 2012). Heteroglossia positions all students as strategic language users (Pacheco & Miller, 2016) and normalizes multilingualism (Machado, 2017). Rosa and Flores (2017a) argue for a raciolinguistic understanding of oral language development. As noted in previous chapters, raciolinguistics recognize the ways in which nonprestigious heritage language learners' linguistic practices are conflated with their racialized, classed bodies. For example, Spanish is valued if White or middle-class people are learning it in immersion schools, but devalued if lower-income people from Mexico and Central America speak it in public spaces. Similarly, while oral language development activities like the ones we will describe allow children to agentically theorize and test ideas, research has shown that children in urban contexts are more often recipients of rigid curricula that promote and reward compliance (Adair et al., 2017).

FOSTERING ORAL LANGUAGE DEVELOPMENT THROUGH TALK AND PLAY

Alicia, Roderick, and Kerry feel that talking in strategic, purposeful ways is the best way to develop oral language. For Alicia, this knowledge also comes with the understanding that the multilingual children she teaches usually have been traumatized by other teachers insisting that they speak only English. Alicia connects with the trauma of being told to deny your own language because she was also told this in school. Yet we know from research that developing children's confidence and knowledge of the content in the language of their family and community is critical (Alvarez, 2012; Valdes et al., 2008). All the teachers attempt to create *playful* spaces, where children freely use their languages through talk, questioning, and conversation. Practices that foster oral language development include morning meeting, sentence stems, interactive read-alouds, think–turn–talk, singing and music, play and games, and multimodal tools.

Morning Meeting

Morning meeting invites children to greet and engage one another in multiple languages in a hybrid manner. Hybridity points to the natural and celebratory mixing and meshing of languages and language varieties to convey meaning. Morning meeting creates a heteroglossic space where all students are users of multiple forms of language (Machado, 2017). Alicia often starts the morning meeting with a child-created question of the day, shared in the morning message. Children develop these questions independently, and many of them have added "and why" to the end of the question to facilitate more conversation. During morning meeting, Kerry and the children often sing popular multilingual folk songs like *Las Ruedas del Autobus* (Spanish translation of

The Wheels on the Bus), *Mi Cuerpo* (Spanish), *La Bella Lavanderina* (Italian), and *One Big Family* (English Sesame Street version), which are widely accessible via YouTube, in the Smithsonian Folkways Folk Music archive (https://folkways.si.edu/), at other websites, such as Books—Multicultural Music Education, and in children's multilingual/cultural song books like *Mi Musica: Somos Latinos* by George Ancona, Alma Flor Ada, and F. Isabel Campoy.

Kerry also tries to foster oral language development through morning meeting conversations and activities related to social studies or science topics. For example, during kindergarten in particular, they work on learning specific words for emotions they might feel throughout the day. Kerry might read aloud books that have photographs of emotions and emotion words under the photo. The photographs help show what the word means because they show the face a child makes when feeling that way; children might be able to remember a time when they've seen someone make that face and the situation they were in and, from the book, know the word for that feeling.

In Roderick's class, in addition to being a hybridized language-using space, morning meeting is also a time for children to share things and ideas they feel are valuable in their lives and communities. During the morning meeting, Roderick is merely the facilitator. For some children, it takes months before they become comfortable enough to join in on these informal morning meeting discussions on their own. But Roderick knows that even observing so much talk helps children's oral language grow tremendously. Children are encouraged to respond to each other by commenting on what their classmates have said or shared or asking a question and then having their own turn to share using sentence stems.

Sentence Stems

The teachers use sentence stems to help children share ideas they feel are meaningful. Sentence stems include:

- Thank you for sharing, I have a connection. . . .
- I like _____.
- Thank you for sharing, I have a question. . . .
- I agree with _____, but I would like to add on. . . .
- I disagree with _____, and I would like to add on. . . .

Alicia provides sentence stems for discussion and debate; they help her students share agreement or disagreement with classmates. Children then develop critical thinking, problem-solving strategies, and listening skills. If Alicia's students want to challenge her or a classmate, they have to be able to first listen and learn from one another. Figure 5.1 shows sentence stems that Alicia uses to foster classroom discussion in morning meeting and beyond.

Figure 5.1. Bilingual (Spanish/English) Sentence Stems

Estoy de acuerdo porque . . . /I agree because . . .
No estoy de acuerdo porque . . . /I do not agree because . . .
En mi opinión . . . /In my opinion . . .
Estoy mí recuerdo de . . . /This reminds me of . . .
Yo pienso que . . . /I think that . . .
Me gusta . . . /I like . . .
No me gustó . . . /I did not like . . .

Kerry teaches children sentence stems for use in resolving conflict, as well. She typically asks children to use "I feel" statements, within this sentence stem:

- I feel _____ when you _____ could you _____?

In response to the "I feel" statement, their classmate might say, "Okay" or "Yes," and if they also want to share something they didn't like that their classmate did, they would repeat the same phrases back. This sentence stem helps children talk about their own feelings, the behavior that prompted them, and what they need to feel better. It helps them do that instead of saying something out of anger, such as "You're mean" or "You're not my friend," which often just escalates the conflict.

Interactive Read-Alouds

As an extension of her morning meeting discussions about emotions, Kerry fosters oral language development by reading books that have stories about children having particular feelings, such as *Sometimes I'm Bombaloo* by Rachel Vail or *On Monday When It Rained* by Cherryl Kachenmeister. She asks children to share a time when they felt a particular emotion described in the books, and if they can't think of a time they felt that way, she might offer a personal example or a hypothetical example that would relate to their personal experiences. Figure 5.2 shares examples of other read-alouds that the teachers use to foster oral language.

Figure 5.2. Read Alouds That Foster Oral Language

I Choose series by Elizabeth Estrada
Sometimes I'm Bombaloo by Rachel Vail
On Monday When It Rained by Cherryl Kachenmeister
I Love Saturdays y Domingos by Alma Flor Ada
Ada Twist, Scientist by Andrea Beaty
¡Solo Pregunta!/Just Ask by Sonia Sotomayor
We All Sing with the Same Voice by J. Phillip Miller and Sheppard M. Greene
Maya's Blanket/La Manta de Maya by Monica Brown

Think-Turn-Talk

The teachers intentionally create time for children to talk to one another and ask questions. Although most teachers use "Turn and Talk," one of the most important parts of this activity is often left out—"Think" (Taberski, 2017). Think–turn–talk fosters oral language development, as children share with one another in response to open-ended questions (Wasik & Iannone-Campbell, 2012). Open-ended questions sound like:

- From what we read, tell your partner what you know.
- What did you learn about ____?
- Why do you think ____ is important?
- Share with your partner.

As they pose open-ended questions, the teachers allow ample time for children to respond (this is important!). Unfortunately, closed questions with known-answers (like "What color [or shape, letter, etc. . . .] is that?") are most common in schools (Heath, 1982; Wasik & Iannone-Campbell, 2012).

Musical Joyfulness

Music joyfully fosters oral language development. For Roderick personally, music is a cultural cornerstone; musical language is vibrant and dynamic. Roderick always plays music in meetings and during transitions. For example, he sometimes plays Naughty by Nature's "Hip Hop Hooray" during the transition between morning meeting and reading workshop. During the transition from lunch, children select the music, ranging from Bachata, Merengue, Merengue Tipico, Reggae, Salsa, Soca, and Haitian to Rap, Reggaeton, and Pop. Prior to using any songs selected by the children, they talk about the language, why they chose the song, the meaning, their favorite parts, and, at times, why some songs might be inappropriate. In the case of them being inappropriate, Roderick discusses why so that children do not feel upset or are embarrassed. Then he plays the instrumental version.

Musical Bookends. On Monday and Friday mornings and afternoons, Roderick creates time during morning meeting and the closing cipher (a closing circle that draws on African community principles) for musical joyfulness. He wants children to have a sense of joy to bookend the beginning and ending of the week. Music helps celebrate the accomplishments of the week and builds excitement for the weekend. During these musical bookends to the week, children can sing and dance in the languages and cultures they love; the joy, pride, and excitement they show is astounding.

Chants. Roderick also playfully develops children's oral language by encouraging them to come up with chants. For example, as transition music ends, children often chant: "Go, go, go, go, go, go, go, go, go, go!" as they gather their materials for the next subject. Also, when children want to show appreciation for something or someone, they share their made-up chant "Ah-berr-berr-berr-berrrrrrr!"

Singing. Like Roderick, Kerry uses music throughout the day. She finds that singing during transitions helps children attend better. For example, while children are cleaning up from an activity, Kerry sings a song her colleague created: "Clean up everybody, clean up everyone. If I help you, and you help me, we'll get this little job done." Kerry's class also sings songs during meetings. One year, Kerry's children were fond of singing "We All Sing with the Same Voice" from Sesame Street. Sometimes Kerry would read the picture book that features this song to children during morning meeting and an interactive read-aloud. It has a very catchy chorus: "We all sing with the same voice, the same song, the same voice. We all sing with the same voice, and we sing in harmony." Kerry asked children to say what they know about the word "harmony." Then they created a motion of two hands interlocking. This song became a class favorite.

Kerry has also sung songs with kids that develop particular phonological awareness skills by creating rhyming words and substituting one phoneme for another. For instance, she sings the American folk song "Jenny Jenkins" which uses color words to describe what Jenny will and won't wear. Kids can then substitute any color word in this song (blue, orange, black, etc.) and any reason that that "Jenny" won't wear that color. The reason has to rhyme with the color; to create the rhyme, they swap out a different initial consonant sound for the color word. The goal is just to play with language while practicing phoneme substitution and rhyming. For example, they could sing, "I won't wear pink because I like to wink," or "because I saw a jink."

Kerry also teaches songs in Spanish to the kids. For kids who already speak Spanish at home, these songs might reinforce vocabulary they already know. For kids who don't speak Spanish, the songs might teach them new vocabulary. One example is "Mi Cuerpo" by Gil Raldiris. This song involves translanguaging—saying different body parts in Spanish and making noise with that body part in English.

Kerry also sings songs that help kids practice clapping syllables in their names and other words. They might sing the words "Say your name and when you do, we will sing it back to you," which is a song Kerry created, or the folk song "Hickety Tickety Bumble Bee, Can you say your name with me?"

Play and Games

Play is a multimodal and communicative human meaning-making event. Through play, children take up important roles; explore and imagine; reflect and share; negotiate shared stories; access and appropriate cultural resources; interpret, create, and reconfigure texts; and engage in meaning-making (Larson & Marsh, 2015; Wohlwend, 2013).

For Alicia, using games is one of the easiest ways to playfully develop heteroglossic oral language; games get children talking across languages. She plays board games, such as checkers, monopoly, and operation with children, or teaches them how to play with one another. Alicia has also used Legos, playdough, and jewelry making as a way of facilitating language development. She finds that in particular, Legos and playdough work so well! Her scholars are given 30–45 minutes with the materials, usually on Fridays, and they play in small groups or independently. One year, three students spent their time over three Fridays creating a Lego city. However, they were missing many of the pieces. Alicia encouraged them to talk with others to work out a plan for sharing materials. They negotiated across languages with classmates to swap pieces to create their vision. They changed their plan several times as well, because as they worked, they realized which pieces could go together and which couldn't. When they finally finished it on the fourth Friday, they asked Alicia for something to cover it with so that they could surprise their classmates with an unveiling! The students were so engaged that they wrote about it later during the writing workshop.

Roderick's class plays board, card, or outside games like hopscotch and hand games. Throughout these engaging activities, he encourages heteroglossic oral language. He says "Speak as though you were talking with cousins, friends or family members using their individual languages and language varieties!" Sometimes Roderick steps in to model or facilitate or to learn for himself. As they play, Roderick hears children let go and show their true selves—it is exhilarating to see! This is the joy in learning Roderick strives to foster.

Kerry teaches kids a game called "Guess My Word," which can help children orally segment and blend words. Kerry shows children a picture card of a mystery word, starting with simple words and moving toward more complex ones. When they play this game, Kerry demonstrates a motion and pronounces the phonemes for the children, and they only do consonant–vowel–consonant (CVC) words (like "sun") or CCVC words (like "flat"), with sounds they have studied and with words kids would be familiar with. For example, for the word/picture of "frog," Kerry says and does the motions and says these phonemes: /f/ /r/ /o/ /g/. Then, the other players have to figure out what word Kerry means. After someone figures out the "mystery word," they all say the sounds and do the motion for the word and then practice blending the sounds.

As you have read, in Kerry's class children have a designated time during the day called work time. During work time, Kerry fosters oral language by sitting with children and describing what they are doing with materials. For example, if someone is rolling clay, she might say, "You're rolling the clay. You're putting your hand on it and making it round all around." Or if someone is pinching, pressing, or smoothing the clay, she might describe that.

Offering this kind of vocabulary helps children attach the word to a concrete action they are doing and understand what the word means. It also helps them learn words that they can use to describe ways they change the shape of the clay. Kerry also helps children learn prepositions by naming what they are doing. She might notice that they are putting a ball of clay "under" another one, or moving a clay figure "through" a little tunnel.

Children in Kerry's class who speak Spanish sometimes also speak Spanish with one another when they are playing, both on their own and with her encouragement. This past year, she remembers two students spoke to one another in Spanish as they worked at neighboring tables with play-dough. Sometimes Kerry speaks Spanish with students to let them know that Spanish is welcome and to encourage them to speak in Spanish if they wish to. Children also use African American Language when they are playing with each other during work time and recess, and Kerry affirms their language.

Multimodal Oral Language Tools

Children engage in a range of multimodal literacy practices and technologies in our digitized world. These tools, used in and outside of school, engage children in becoming text producers, critics, and tinkerers (Lankshear & Knobel, 2004; Luke & Freebody, 1999). The teachers tap into these tools to foster oral language. Roderick engages children in writing and recording videos of their work in English and in their heritage language or language varieties. He invites children to share these writings and videos with their families and to compare and contrast the languages. The *I Am Enough* project described in the opening vignette led children to create multimodal texts using a variety of materials. After creating their texts, children recorded videos about them using Clips and Flipgrid, which are free applications that are allowed on their school-issued iPads.

Alicia also uses Flipgrid as a tool for children to use to record themselves. For example, on January 7, 2021, the day after the insurrection at the nation's capital, children spent the majority of morning meeting talking, discussing, reading, and sharing their feelings. Many didn't say anything; they just listened. Alicia wanted all children to be able to express something, whether it was a feeling they had or that they did not understand what happened. Children were able to independently share through a Flipgrid video without the pressure of anyone watching them. Alicia also uses Flipgrid for other open-ended topics, and children seemed to respond well to it. For example, children made Flipgrids based on an interview with their families about their families' favorite music.

Alicia has also discovered the power of voice recordings. She has had children record themselves answering questions about books as they read during independent reading time. She has also had children record themselves having natural conversations. They are able to play it back and hear themselves talking across multiple languages and language varieties. Alicia has also used voice recordings to record herself reading a story in order to model fluency. She also thinks audiobooks are important so that children are able to hear what the words on the page sound like (and research confirms this practice!). She integrates audiobooks into independent reading time in her classroom.

VOCABULARY DEVELOPMENT

Vocabulary is a critical component of oral language development and develops in tandem with it. Children are biologically wired to learn receptive and expressive vocabulary (Chomsky, 1957; Stahl et al., 2019). This is demonstrated by children "fast mapping" the word meanings, as in the way babies often call all four-legged animals "dog." Receptive language involves recalling, naming, or labeling vocabulary. Expressive language involves describing, storying, and dialoguing. The way Roderick asked children to think about ways they *were enough* developed both their receptive and expressive vocabulary. Children had to understand the meaning of *enough* in order to describe it (Manyak et al., 2021; Stahl et al., 2019).

Receptive and expressive vocabulary are connected to breadth and depth in vocabulary knowledge-building. Breadth involves surface-level knowledge of different words gained through exposure. Breadth is important for decoding, because the more children are exposed to words in school, the more they notice those words when practicing reading. Depth involves understanding the meaning of a word and is key to reading engagement and comprehension (Ouellete, 2006). If readers understand the meaning of a word they encounter while reading, then they are more likely to feel engaged with that text. This connects to why Alicia, Roderick, and Kerry strive to culturally mediate instruction by using children's cultural referents to build vocabulary breadth and depth. They do so through multifaceted vocabulary instruction that is contextualized within heritage knowledge.

Multifaceted vocabulary instruction happens throughout the day and focuses on both explicitly teaching Tier 1, 2, and 3 vocabulary words and teaching strategies to figure out those words (Beck et al., 2013; Manyak et al., 2021). Tier 1, or high-frequency words, are irregular words that children need to memorize and know by "sight" (e.g., Fry's [1980] 300 words). Once high-frequency words are committed to memory, they become sight words (McKenna & Stahl, 2015). Tier 2 words describe simple concepts in a more complex way—"distraught" instead of "sad." Tier 3 words are low-frequency, discipline-specific words like "environmental catastrophe."

Children can learn about 3,000 word families (or more!) each year in school (Graves, 2016). That means teachers need to introduce children to new Tier 1, Tier 2, and Tier 3 words each week and to teach them strategies to figure out new words they encounter as they read (Beck et al., 2013; Graves, 2016; Silverman et al., 2015). There are three dimensions of multifaceted vocabulary instruction: quality, quantity, and strategy.

Quality vocabulary instruction involves explicit and robust teaching of target or Tier 2 and 3 vocabulary words to develop vocabulary depth. The most widely known way to find Tier 2 and 3 words involves weekly selecting and teaching 10–15 words that are widely used, but are more complex ways of describing concepts. Tier 2 and 3 words are context-based. Words that are meaningful for one child may not be meaningful for another.

Quantity instruction focuses on breadth—surrounding children in a sea of words and talk throughout the day. As students encounter and learn about words through efficient explanations of word meanings in context, their vocabulary knowledge develops.

Strategy instruction involves teaching strategies to figure out the meanings of unknown words, like using morphemic parts and context clues (Manyak et al., 2021; Wise, 2022).

However, most vocabulary researchers do not discuss how quality, quantity, and strategy instruction might use and sustain children's cultures and languages. In fact, most discuss how children from lower socioeconomic groups and those who speak languages other than English—like the children in Alicia, Roderick, and Kerry's schools—don't know as many words as their peers. Studies of vocabulary that deem poor children and families as having a "word or language gap" mis-recognize and ignore the value of oral narrative and other valued literacy practices in poor communities (Miller & Sperry, 2012). These studies also fail to mention that White students have access to learning that is active and promotes dynamic, agentive learning (Adair et al., 2017; Genishi & Dyson, 2009). CSP values "new linguistically and culturally dexterous ways of being" (Paris & Alim, 2014, p. 91). CSPs move beyond viewing heritage cultural and community practices as deficits or mere cultural resources to be considered. Instead, CSPs take up the dynamic and shifting ways cultural and linguistic practices are constantly evolving. Next, we think through ways teachers sustain their students' rich and hybridized vocabulary practices, including interactive read-alouds and word/semantic maps, word/graffiti walls, word sorts, reader's theater, and interactive vocabulary development.

Interactive Read-Alouds

Decades of research notes the importance of reading rich children's literature aloud to teach vocabulary (Graves, 2016). By reading multiple genres and engaging children in texts, effective teachers advance quantity vocabulary instruction. Alicia, Roderick, and Kerry introduce big, important Tier 2 and 3 vocabulary words at morning meeting or before they begin reading a new book during reading workshop. Although there are no official lists of Tier 2 vocabulary words, researchers suggest using your "teacher judgement" to identify 10–15 words per week based on knowledge of the children and the selected book (Manyak et al., 2021). It's also key to select vocabulary that is important, relevant, and interesting to children. By teaching vocabulary explicitly, children can learn hundreds of Tier 2 and 3 words a year (Taberski, 2017).

An example of quality vocabulary teaching through interactive read-alouds occurred when Kerry's 1st-grade class talked about fairness. She first asked students what they thought the word *fair* meant. Then, she read *Big Red Lollipop* by Rukhsana Khan, which addresses the issue in the context of a story about siblings learning to share. She followed up this read-aloud by sharing a story she created on a Google Slide about two classmates—one who had glasses and one who didn't. The classmate who didn't need glasses said, "That's not fair. I want glasses, too." The word "fair" was a Tier 2 word that the kindergarteners were still learning. Her goal was not necessarily for children to master the word, but to introduce it. She then noticed that as she and the children discussed the word throughout the day and in different contexts, they began to use "fair" in their own talk.

Although it is important for teachers to pre-identify target words, studies note how important it is for children to identify their own vocabulary words (Graves, 2016). This fosters agentic learning, in which children make their own decisions about what is academically, socially, emotionally, cognitively, culturally, and physically relevant and sustaining. In this way, children test their emerging ideas about words, which builds cognitive capacity (Adair et al., 2017). For example, one year during a bilingual read-aloud of the story *Abuela*, two children in Alicia's class wrote words they wanted to learn more about on sticky notes. When a child wondered about the meaning of the word *mar*, Alicia taught the child how to locate the word's meaning by using context clues:

Dante: The word I wrote is "mar." I think it means something with the sea because of the picture.
Alicia: How do you know they are by the sea?/¿Cómo sabes que están junto al mar?
Alicia: Beautiful. Perfecto. Even if you covered up the words you can tell what is happening by looking at the pictures.

Alicia also teaches children how to figure out a word's meaning by looking at the morphemes or parts of words; for example, by asking a child to cover up the "ed" in the word "docked" (Nash et al., 2022). This is an example of morphemic strategy instruction (Manyak et al., 2021).

The teachers also use interactive and multilingual read-alouds for quantity vocabulary instruction. By choosing texts that connect to children's languages, cultures, and lived experiences, children are able to more deeply and actively connect to the vocabulary. For example, Kerry's class read *This Is Our House* by Michael Rosen and introduced the words, "excluded" and "exclusion" to name what the character was doing. The children could relate to this book, because they, like the lead character, had been building structures during recess and having problems making room for other kids. This story took place in a city, in a playground at the center of a housing complex with high-rise buildings like the ones some of her students live in.

I Am Enough

The teachers also create spaces for children to build vocabulary about their sociopolitical context and help them to understand and become text critics who discuss issues of race, gender, class, and disability (Luke & Freebody, 1999). It might be in response to a comment or something happening in the world. For example, Kerry read aloud the bilingual book *One of a Kind, Like Me/ Único Como Yo* by Laurin Mayeno, which explores the issue of gender identity through the lens of the child Danny/Danielito when she heard children making fun of a child who wanted to pretend to be a girl (Elson & Nash, 2020). Kerry also read the book *Our Skin* by Megan Maddison, Jessica Ralli, and Isabel Roxas to talk about how melanin creates skin color and to talk with children about racism based on concerns about how some children were internalizing racism, reflected in comments like "I don't like that Black kid." Alicia engaged children in comparisons of the books *If Dominican Were a Color* by Sili Recio, *The Colors of Us* by Karén Katz, and *My Many Colored Days* by Dr. Seuss. Children discussed how Seuss's book used black and brown to describe "sad, low, angry, lonely" feelings, while the other two books described vibrant and positive Black and Brown people and things. Then children selected a color that represented them, and created an identity vocabulary map using Google Slides (see Figure 5.3).

Word Walls

Roderick's go-to methods for teaching vocabulary to 2nd- and 3rd-graders involve using index cards connected by rings. Whenever they see or hear a word they do not yet know, they write the word in the vocabulary book,

Figure 5.3. Identity Vocabulary Map

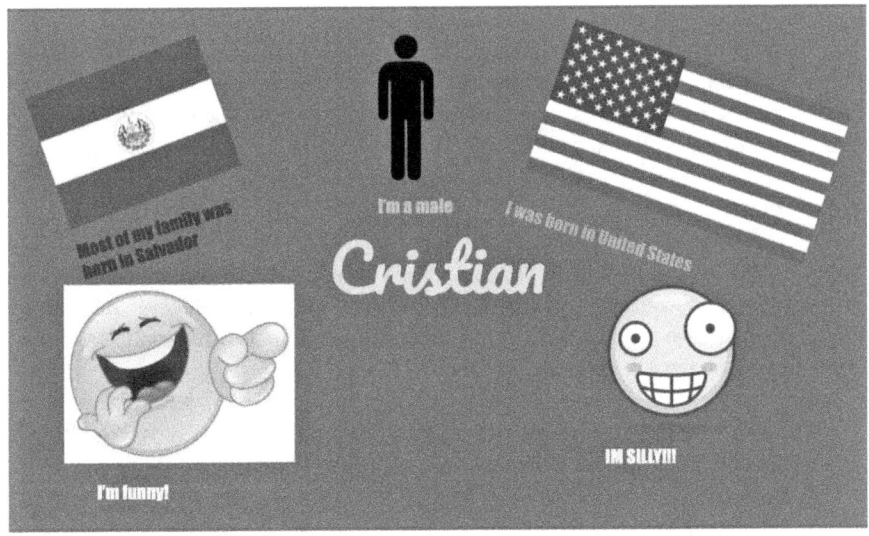

using a computerized or paper dictionary to write the word's definition. Each card can have only one word along with its meaning. Their task is then to connect as many of the new words to their reading and writing each day. Throughout the day, students take "quick vocab breaks" to share words "that make them feel good to learn." This practice of writing down words is vital and supported by research in vocabulary instruction—children need to know the meanings of new words they are learning (Graves, 2016). Twice a week, they add words to their Graffiti Wall, a black-papered bulletin board with vocabulary written in metallic ink (see Figure 5.4).

Alicia and Kerry also have word books and word walls in their classrooms. Kerry's word wall contains high-frequency words (Tier 1 words), and children also have a copy of these words in their writing notebooks. One year, Kerry created a chart to record Tier 2 and 3 thematic vocabulary words that children learned based on their interests in puppets. Children recorded new words they learned through fieldtrips, guest speakers, and touching artifacts about puppets. Kerry also made a center during work time where students could touch, draw, and play with a variety of puppets she created in a college class. Kerry also arranged a visit from an acquaintance who was a puppeteer for *Sesame Street* and took children to see a puppet show at the Central Park Marionette Theater. At the theater, they spoke with the performers afterward and learned about how they used marionettes and a zip line, among other tools, to do the show. From all of these activities, children learned and applied words like *animatronics, zip line, marionette,* and *green screen*.

Alicia's Spanish/English word wall is entirely constructed by children. They are responsible for adding new and interesting vocabulary words. One of the expectations when they add a word to the word wall is that they add a symbol, drawing, or some kind of illustration to describe the word. Drawing symbols or other pictures to go along with vocabulary words helps children internalize their meaning (Manyak et al., 2021).

Word walls provide a reference for children to learn and apply the vocabulary they are learning over time. Because children typically learn new Tier 2 words after at least three exposures, they might decide to "retire" some vocabulary words from their Word Wall when they have internalized them (Taberski, 2017).

Word Sorts

Word sorts are another way that teachers help foster children's vocabulary knowledge. Through sorting words, children acquire and integrate new word knowledge. There are different types of word sorts, including sound, pattern, and meaning sorts (Bear et al., 2012):

- **Sound sorts**—sorting pictures by initial sound, rhyme, consonant blends or digraphs, syllables, or accented syllables
- **Pattern sorts**—sorting words into word families (hat, rat, pat or ran, tan, pan)

I Am Enough

Figure 5.4. Graffiti Wall and Word Books

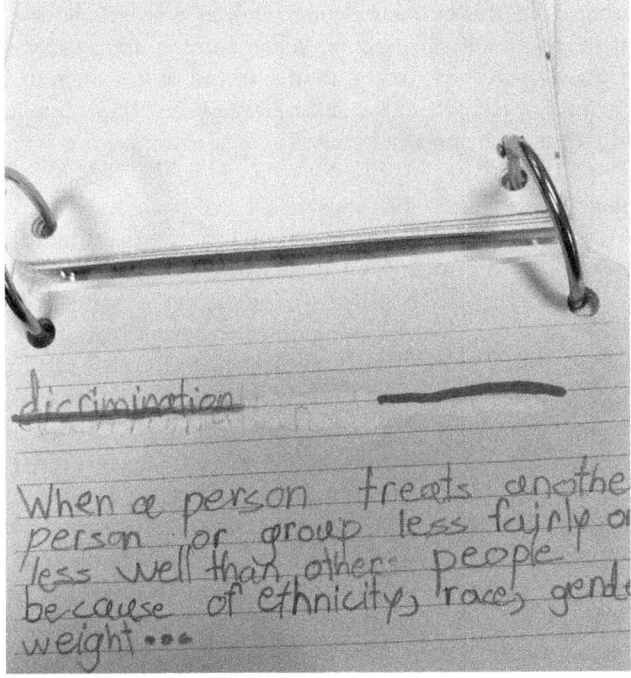

- **Meaning sorts**—sorting objects or pictures or words by concepts. This is a good way to link vocabulary instruction with conceptual understanding and is often used in content-area teaching (e.g., group all of the pictures of mammals).

Word sorts can be closed or open, teacher-directed or independent. Open sorts require the highest independent effort. With student-centered open sorts, children are given a set of words or letters relevant to their current studies and asked to come up with a way to sort them. Sorts can also be done with partners (Bear et al., 2012).

Reader's Theater

Reader's Theater is an activity where children read a text as a performance for the class. It's a helpful strategy for vocabulary, fluency, and comprehension (Taberski, 2017). This strategy is particularly important for children who may have a hard time with reading, because they can read their lines with someone. The teachers do Reader's Theater activities in the moment or as planned, encouraging children to practice reading, making sure they are using their voices expressively for a later performance. Kerry has taught children vocabulary through Reader's Theater. One year, she used Reader's Theater activities in the moment while reading a story about a chipmunk family, *Math Tricks* by Kathy Schulz. When coming upon the word *burrow*, the student wasn't sure how to pronounce it and didn't seem to know what the word meant. So, Kerry and the children read the other sentences together with lots of expression and used context clues to figure out what the word meant.

Kerry also enacts Reader's Theater by encouraging children to make puppet shows with one or two other classmates at work time. Kerry invites them to make a setting and the puppets out of paper, write their story, rehearse the story with each other, and then act out the story for their classmates during share time. Making and performing a puppet show gives children a chance to practice speaking and listening to each other and to their classmates. They need to suggest ideas for the show to their partner, orally come up with the story, and then write a script, which can help them remember their idea. Orally telling the story and sharing ideas helps children practice their expressive (storying) and receptive (naming) vocabulary. Performing the show gives children a chance to practice speaking clearly and loudly enough that everyone understands what is happening. The teachers have also printed out favorite poems or texts and worked with kids for about 5–10 minutes each day during morning meeting or reader's workshop to practice reading their parts expressively (for example, *I, Too, Am America* by Langston Hughes, which works well because each child can share one or two lines of the short poem). Gradually, the children practice their lines until they are ready to perform, talking about new vocabulary together as they read expressively. When children are ready to perform, families are invited to attend, or the performance is recorded. Teaching vocabulary through Reader's Theater centers children's voices and creates ownership and agency in the learning process.

Interactive Vocabulary Development

Roderick has used hopscotch and hand games to interactively teach vocabulary while creating affirming learning spaces. Roderick introduced children to hopscotch, since there was a hopscotch path painted on the blacktop. One day, children were divided into three heterogeneous groups to play the game and were given the direction that everyone must encourage and give advice about how to reach the stone. This was helpful for expressive and receptive vocabulary and social development. He also asks scholars to share hand games. Hand games or hand jives (e.g., Miss Mary Mack) are cultural traditions that come from the Black community (Baines et al., 2018). Engaging children in hand games elevates the collective experiences of many Black women and girls and engages children in beat-making. The Black Girls Handgames Project (www.handgamesproject.com/) is one resource that Roderick uses to incorporate this method of experiential and musically interactive vocabulary instruction.

Kerry helps children develop vocabulary by teaching them hand motions for certain words. Often when singing a new song, when Kerry's students get to a word they don't know, Kerry might ask children if anyone can say what they know about the word. She then adds more information if needed. Then she might ask students to come up with hand motions that we could do when that word comes up in the song. Sometimes she might combine two or three children's ideas to create a hand motion that matches the meaning of the word. Talking about the definition and creating and doing these hand motions can help children remember what the word means.

The way the teachers teach vocabulary in context through interactive activities is consistent with extensive research on vocabulary. Children do not learn vocabulary through merely memorizing or recording definitions from a dictionary. No research to date supports teaching vocabulary in isolation (Beck et al., 2013).

CONCLUSION: I AM ENOUGH

Culturally sustaining approaches to oral language and vocabulary development can redefine the ways educators conceptualize culture in oral language development and vocabulary learning. CSPs position culture language as hybrid and dynamic, talking back to deficit notions. In that way, CSPs "attempt to reimagine minoritized linguistic practices not simply as starting points but rather as central components of all stages of learning across contexts" (Rosa & Flores, 2017b, p. 178). As this chapter has detailed, culturally sustaining approaches to oral language and vocabulary development are hybrid, heteroglossic, and dynamic. They engage children in agentically exploring language—which leads them to a place where they know *I am enough*.

CHAPTER 6

"Just Because My Parents Are From El Salvador You Can't Say They Are Bad and Evil"
Culturally Sustaining Ways of Writing

*Kindel Turner Nash, Alicia Arce-Boardman,
Roderick Peele, and Kerry Elson*

Dear Donald Trump,

> Do you even know where I am from? I am from El Salvador. Just because you're white it doesn't mean that you have to send us back. Do you know how long it took my parents to come here? We came here for a better life. Just because my parents are from El Salvador you can't say they are bad and evil. I wonder where you learned this. Do your parents know you do this? I hope you're not president. Shame on you. Mr. Donald Trump I don't like you. I wish you didn't do this never.

Alicia, Roderick, and Kerry strive to create critical classroom spaces that "allow young children and practitioners to engage in discursive situations and practices within their lives" (Wynter-Hoyte et al., 2019, p. 434). They believe that classrooms need to be spaces to identify, name, and interrupt systems of oppression (Boutte & Muller, 2018). Before and during the Trump presidency, many families in the largely immigrant communities where Alicia, Roderick, Kerry, and their students live were faced with anti-immigrant discourse, creating a palpable sense of fear.

Vasquez (2014) writes "how we choose to teach, the decisions that we make, are political decisions" (p. 8). In response to children's fears and

---

Focus Questions: What does current research say about how children learn to write? In what ways can teachers implement culturally sustaining writing practices?

concerns about President Trump's anti-immigrant discourse, Alicia decided to read the book *Separate Is Never Equal: Sylvia Mendez and Her Family's Fight for Desegregation* by Duncan Tonatiuh. This book tells the story of a young Brown girl from Mexico, Sylvia Mendez, and her families' efforts to integrate an all-White school. Echoing President Trump's xenophobic discourse, on her first day, a White boy yells at Sylvia to "Go back to the Mexican School. You don't belong here!" Alicia was deeply sensitive to her students' feelings—people in her family were having similar anxieties. Instead of letting the discussion end with creating a space to process feelings, Alicia asked, "What do you want to do?" Students said, "We should send Trump a letter." You read part of one child's letter at the onset of this chapter.

Previous chapters have discussed the efforts that teachers make to get to know families and communities and to make the classroom a space where kids, as social and cultural beings, can thrive as readers and multilingual communicators. In the example above, Alicia linked her deep knowledge of the children within their multidimensional ecological community system (see Figure 1.3) to foster writing not just for ability, but also for liberation.

In this chapter, we focus on culturally sustaining writing teaching processes and practices like the letter to Trump. We discuss hybridized writing workshops, interactive and group writing, and handwriting. We begin with an overview of current research in writing, including frameworks rooted in critical sociocultural and culturally sustaining theories.

HOW DO CHILDREN LEARN TO WRITE?

By the time children arrive in school, they are already authors within their social and cultural worlds. In their homes and communities, they take the stage, tell stories about their own identities and experiences, and showcase complex pragmatic, semantic, and syntactic understandings of language through marks and drawings (Bentley & Souto-Manning, 2019). Writing is the activity during which authors *get words on the page*—communicating or composing using an orthographic print system (Ray & Cleaveland, 2008). It is intimately connected with reading and talking and is fashioned by our social and cultural relationships (Dyson, 2013). Ann Haas Dyson's extensive research on literacy development in children's cultures highlights the idea that "language is based in reciprocal relations" (2013, p. 6). People do not learn to write by "crafting proper language in isolation from the world" but by "responding to others as active participants in the world as we know it" (Dyson, 2013, p. 7; Purcell-Gates et al., 2011). As Vygotsky (1978) says, our minds take shape in society. Across languages and language varieties, writing develops in similar ways.

Writing development should not be confused with handwriting or other procedural aspects of writing such as learning to write your own name (Quinn & Bingham, 2019). Handwriting is forming the letters of the orthographic system correctly. It requires a certain degree of self-regulation and fine motor skills (Chandler et al., 2021). While research notes the importance of teaching children to write their names and handwriting (Chandler et al., 2021; Maldarelli et al., 2015), too often, writing in early childhood is overly focused on these tasks (Puranik & Lonigan, 2011).

Some research on how children learn to write mirrors research about how children learn to read. Stage and repertoire models of writing and composing suggest that children progress through fluid stages as they acquire writing abilities, skills, and strategies (Clay, 2013; Dyson, 2013; Sulbzy & Teale, 1991; Templeton, 2020). Researchers differentiate between stages of writing, composing, and spelling development. Although we see children's writing as traversing fluid stages or repertoires, we are cautious about viewing stages of writing development as fixed. Fundamentally, we see literacy learning as an active and reciprocal process grounded in children's and communities' ways of knowing and being. This is why we visualize literacy learning as a hyperbolic plane—an organic figure with many simultaneous inputs and outputs rather than a line of regression (Nash & Piña, 2020) (see Figure 1.2). Thinking about writing development as a fixed set of stages is a Western, analytical way of thinking (Nash & Piña, 2020) that does not accurately describe the holistic and communal ways of knowing, being, and *writing* that are at play as children learn to write (see Figure 6.1). This vision of writing development is one way to divest from Whiteness, as first and foremost, culturally sustaining pedagogy "explicitly names Whiteness (including white normativity, white

Figure 6.1. Ways of Knowing, Being, and Writing

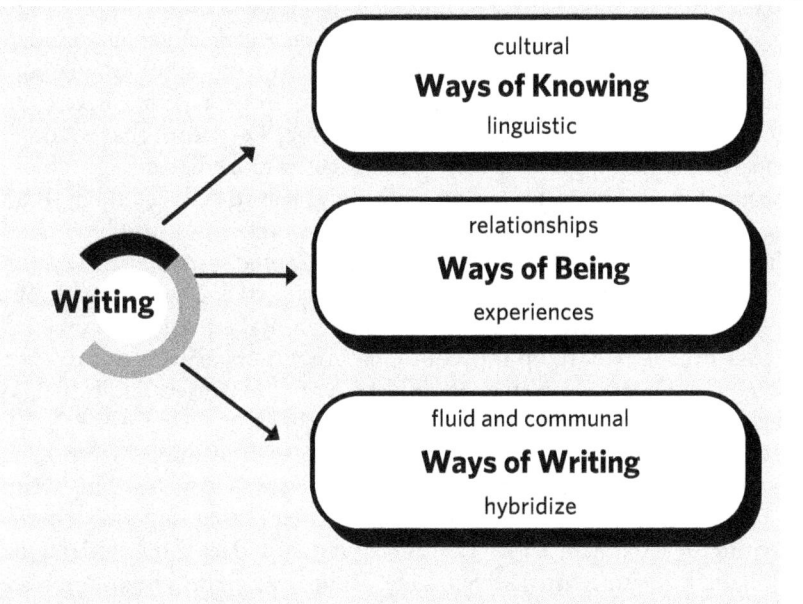

racism and ideologies of white supremacy) as the problem, and thus, decentering whiteness and recentering communities is our point of departure" (Paris, 2021, p. 368). Bakhtin's (1984) notion of hybridity is particularly important to our thinking about ways of writing. Hybridity, or meshing, mixing, talking, writing, and drawing across multiple languages and language varieties, contributes to a rich tapestry of textual meaning-making (Machado, 2017, p. 311). For example, when multilingual children like those in in Alicia's, Roderick's, and Kerry's classrooms use the written systems of multiple languages and/or language varieties simultaneously, rather than being confused, they actively investigate multiple graphic symbols, integrating knowledge of the languages into their writing (Dyson, 2013; Gillanders, 2018).

Because "anticipating an audience is a fundamental aspect of communication of any sort" (Dyson, 2013, p. 51)—but is especially true of writing—appreciating the communal, hybrid, communicative function of writing is especially important to Alicia, Roderick, and Kerry as they create writing engagements that are culturally sustaining.

Thus, the stages of writing, composing, and spelling described below should be viewed as fluid and overlapping and as informed by children's linguistic and cultural contexts, as well as by the relationships children form as they share their ideas in the "textual playground" of the classroom (Dyson, 2013, p. 8).

Fluid Stages of Writing

As noted in previous chapters, the English orthographic system is complex: the letters that we have (26) aren't enough to represent all the sounds (42–44, or more, depending on language varieties. There are 20 vowel sounds, but only 6 vowels. English has many words adopted from other languages, and we use fossilized spellings (Share, 2008). Yet, from a young age, children demonstrate powerful understandings of writing. They learn that writing represents things, that in most Western languages it looks like straight lines and goes from left to right, and that words have spaces in between them (Puranik & Lonigan, 2011). Decades of research shows the ways in which children begin to demonstrate knowledge of the orthographic system and the relationship between oral and written language (Clay, 2013; Dyson, 2013; Sulzby & Teale, 1991; Templeton, 2020). As children make marks to make meaning, over time they develop into more mature writers. This is not to say that drawing is replaced by writing; as children write, they insert additional layers in their "multimodal story-making" (Dyson, 2013, p. 51). Table 6.1 defines and displays examples of fluid writing stages, with examples from Kindel's own children and kindergarten students from Kerry's class (scribble writing).

These examples of flexible, organic, and intersecting stages or repertoires of writing development show children's gradually deepening understanding of alphabetic writing. At the beginning of the year, many children in Kerry's kindergarten class may be engaging in scribble writing (as in the crayon

Just Because My Parents Are From El Salvador 93

Table 6.1. Fluid Stages of Writing

Drawing as Representation: Writing as pictures and marks	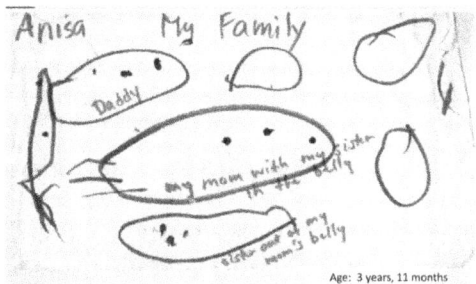 Age: 3 years, 11 months
Scribble Writing: Writing as lines	 Age: 5 years, 1 mo.
Mock Letters: Writing as letter-like shapes	 Age: 4 years, 3 months
Writing own name or strings of letters: Writing with pictures, marks, lines, and letters	 Age: 4 years, 3 months

writing in Table 6.1), but they are *also* able to write their own names. Other children may write mock letters, *and* some letters of their own names (of course, their name's letters are usually very familiar!). Typically by the time children come to Alicia and Roderick's 2nd- and 3rd-grade classrooms, they have progressed through these stages.

Developing Writerly Selves: Composition Development

Regardless of whether children are drawing representative pictures or attempting to write letters, they are authors or composers. Every image that a child creates holds important meaning for that particular child at that particular moment. This is why in prekindergarten and kindergarten, teachers often transcribe what young children have to say about what they have composed, as in the first image in Table 6.1.

Kerry doesn't typically transcribe directly on the child's writing. Instead, she usually writes the child's words on a sticky note or on the back of the paper. Transcribing children's thoughts is a way to hold on to the child's meaning-making that happens during the composing event until they are able to hold that meaning for themselves. For example, in Dana Bentley's pre-K classroom, children gradually moved from drawing, with teachers transcribing their stories, to thinking about ways they might use letters to write their own stories. Bentley helped move children in this direction by bringing them to a morning meeting and saying "Many people want to write stories . . . but there aren't enough teachers to do all the writing." Children then offered suggestions, such as "You just listen to the word and then hear the letters." "Yeah, the teachers, but also some of the kids can help spell things" (Bentley & Souto-Manning, 2019, p. 124).

Composition development, or as Alicia says, developing a writerly self, runs parallel to, but isn't the same as writing and spelling development (Ray & Glover, 2008). Fluid stages of composing can be seen in the way children progressively:

- engage in writing to represent what they mean,
- write about topics that are interesting to them,
- remain focused on writing,
- engage in revision, and
- share their texts with others (Ray & Glover, 2008).

Alicia, Roderick, and Kerry observe children moving in and out and across writing and composition development as they ensure that the classroom surrounds children in a meaningful flood of language, ask meaningful questions during writing time, help children develop stamina, write interactively with children, use child-created labels throughout the classroom, engage in mini-lessons and think-alouds about writing, and study mentor texts and notice the features of writing in those books (Bentley & Souto-Manning, 2019).

Fluid Stages of Spelling

While writing and composing is about learning to get ideas and words down on paper, spelling growth involves learning to represent language patterns in writing (Bear et al., 2012). Scholars also recognize progressive and fluid stages of spelling development: letter name, within-word, syllables and affixes, and derivational (Bear et al., 2012). Table 6.2 displays spelling stages with some examples in Spanish, African American Language, and Dominant English (translations are provided in brackets where appropriate). It is important to note that if children are multilingual and/or have multiple language varieties, their spelling development will logically reflect aspects of their multiple languages and language varieties (Dyson, 2013; Gillanders, 2018).

Table 6.2. Fluid Stages of Spelling

Early Letter-Name Alphabetic Spelling	ISDDR [I saw the deer.]
Spelling the first and last sound of words with consonants. Often lacks spacing between words. This is sometimes called "invented spelling."	VLBNAD0 [Vi el venado.]
Middle Letter-Name Alphabetic Spelling	I be pecan fars.
Spelling the first and last sounds of words with consonants, digraphs, and some middle vowel sounds and a few high-frequency words.	Estoy recogendo flores.
	I am pecan fars.
	[I am picking flowers.]
Late Letter-Name Alphabetic Spelling	I jupt out the jet.
Spelling that consistently uses regular short vowel sounds, digraphs, and consonant blends. Can spell some high-frequency words.	Solté del jet.
	I jupt out of the jet.
	[I jumped out of the jet.]
Within-Word Pattern Spelling	We goin to florda and we mite swim.
Correctly spelling most one-syllable short vowel words, consonant blends, digraphs, and preconsonantal nasals (like m in bump). Spell many high-frequency words and words with consonant–vowel–consonant (CVC) patterns.	We are goin to florda and we mite swim.
	Nosotros vamos a flarida y podriamos nedar.
	[We are going to Florida and we might go to the beach and swim.]
Syllables and Affixes Spelling	We went out west last sumer. We drove a littel camper bus. We steyed in alot of Nashal Parks and went hiking in the mountains. It was relly cool.
Spelling many multisyllabic words and considering spelling patterns where syllables and morphemes meet (prefixes and suffixes).	
Derivational Relations Spelling	Math homework is usually okay. It's been mostly easy and some challaging. The hardest part is devision.
Spelling that demonstrates understanding that words are derived from base and root words or morphemes.	

Fluid stages of writing and spelling generally line up with the fluid stages of reading noted in Chapter 4 (pre-alphabetic, partial alphabetic, full alphabetic, and consolidated alphabetic) (Bear et al., 2012). However, learning to spell, like learning to read, write, and compose, is dynamic and fluid. For example, a child in Roderick's 2nd-grade class who was using within-word spelling patterns in their writing (e.g., "nabere's haws" [neighbor's house]), was also beginning to utilize some syllables and affixes (e.g., the -ing in "hopeing" and the "'s" in "nabere's"). Spelling development is also shaped within the context of a child's languages and cultures. This is reflected in the child's use of grammatical and pragmatic features of African American language in the phrase "nex wut hapine" [next what happened] (see Figure 6.2).

Figure 6.2. Within-Word Pattern/Syllables and Affixes Spelling

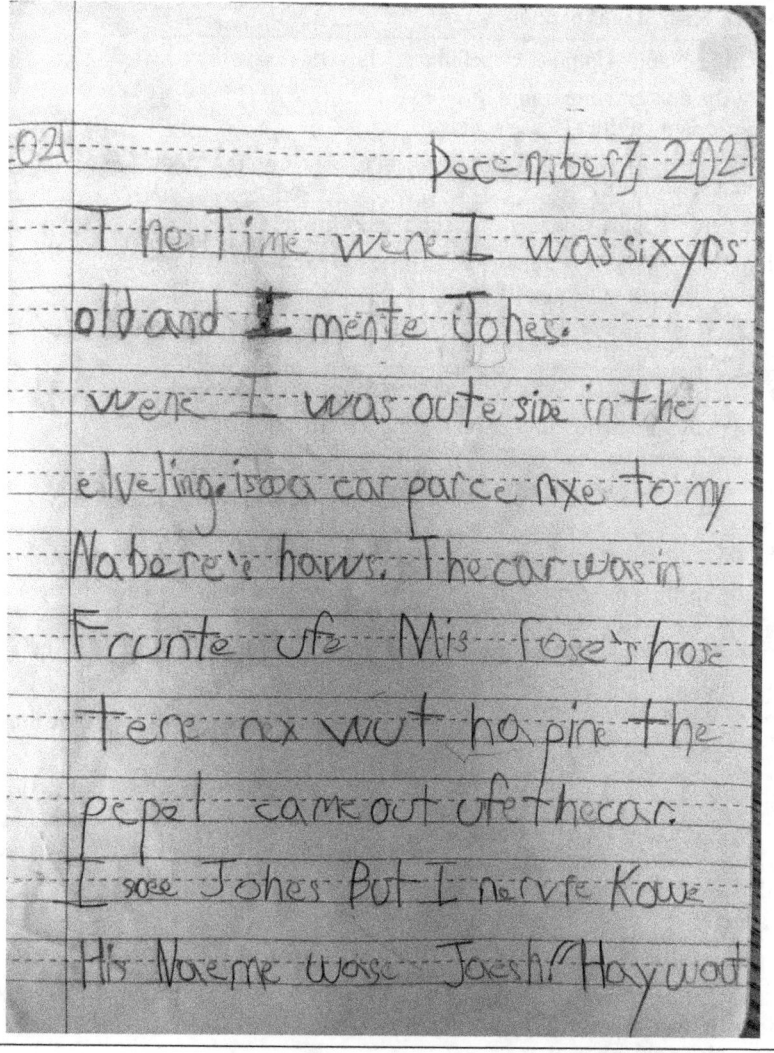

CULTURALLY SUSTAINING WRITING INSTRUCTION

Alicia, Roderick, and Kerry strive to make writing meaningful, culturally sustaining, and life-affirming. To do so, they critically center children's languages through encouraging code-meshing, contrastive analysis, and translanguaging. They incorporate children's input and voices. They work, through their writing instruction, to help children be in right relationship with the land and provide children with structured opportunities to contend with injustice (Paris, 2020). As with the letters to Trump, through writing children become policy critiquers, change-agents, and problem-posers (Friere, 1972). These activities allow children to "talk back" (Kinloch, 2010), "refigure identities . . . and assert agency" through writing (Kinloch, 2011, p. 2).

To foster cultural sustenance, they *hybridize* writing processes and practices within children's cultures, creating spaces where children fuse, mix, and remix diverse threads of their language, social, and media worlds into everyday writing (Dyson, 2013). Grounded in ideas about hybridized writing in children's cultures, we now share culturally sustaining writing practices from the teachers' classrooms. Specifically, we share examples of hybridized and culturally sustaining writing workshops, interactive and group writing experiences, and word study/handwriting.

Hybridized Writing Workshop

In order for children to develop their ways of writing, they must be in multimodal spaces with protected writing time nearly every day. As you read in Chapter 3, the teachers call their writing time "writing workshop" (Graves, 1983). Writing workshop facilitates the *writing process*. The writing process describes the recursive way that writers take what they know from the "rhythm and rhymes" of their lives through a process of writing, revising, editing, and publishing (Genishi & Dyson, 2009, p. 20). The teachers don't race toward publishing, because the process is as important as the product (Bentley & Souto-Manning, 2019). Writing workshop is a space where Alicia, Roderick, and Kerry can teach children to love writing through centering their voices and languages in the writing process. It is a space where children create real books, just like the writers and illustrators of the books they read. They have found that when the writing time has purpose and is fun, multimodal, multilingual, and informal, children become excited about telling and sharing their stories and ideas-cultivating "we-ness" (Dyson, 2013). *Hybridizing* the writing workshop ensures that multilingual and language-variety speakers have a flexible space to make multiple meanings in multiple ways.

The hybridized writing workshop time varies depending on the year, but it always has three parts:

1. **Mini-lesson:** 10-minute lesson to teach content
2. **Writing/Conferring:** 15–45-minute block of time during which children work on writing guided by choice. Teachers work with small groups and/or confer with children.

3. **Share time:** 5–10 minutes at the end of the block. Teacher selects or children volunteer to share what they have learned.

The following is what happens during each part of the workshop.

Mini-lesson. The mini-lesson is with all the children together. The teachers teach a new skill or strategy, such as coming up with an idea for a book or adding dialogue to a realistic fiction story, and then give children time to briefly practice the skill or strategy. Alicia uses Seravallo's (2017) *The Writing Strategies Book* as a resource for her mini-lessons, selecting strategies and skills based on her observations and assessments of children's writing. The mini-lesson time in the classrooms remains 10 minutes or less all year, unless the teachers start it by reading a text by a mentor author. Sometimes mini-lesson skills and strategies might be outlined in a schoolwide curriculum or in state or national writing standards. For example, aligned with the 2nd-grade standards for personal narrative writing, Alicia did a mini-lesson about how sometimes bilingual writers write a personal narrative with a beginning, middle, and end. Then, in independent writing, students created "quilt pieces" about family cultural traditions—like church days, Christmas, and going to El Salvador—across languages and language varieties based on interviews they conducted with a family member or elder (see Figure 6.3). What makes this writing activity hybridized and culturally sustaining is that the focus is on multilingualism and learning from families and elders—and this was not a one-time lesson, it is part of Alicia's ongoing efforts to engage children in writing that is life-affirming.

Independent Writing. During independent writing, teachers usually start by observing the whole class for a few minutes and supporting children who may need additional help. Because of their deep understanding of their students' cultural and linguistic practices, they strive to foster interdependence—learning and working together—during this time (Harlin & Souto-Manning, 2009). In that way, "independent writing" time in the teachers' classrooms isn't individualistic, it's collectivistic. The teachers feel that students learn better from each other. Collectivity is important to the teachers, because the teachers are concerned about popular ideas about writing workshop instruction that to compose, one must go inward and obtain everything from within, when in reality people make meaning from talking, writing, and reading with others (Dyson, 2013). For example, as Roderick's students wrote realistic fictional narratives based on *My First Trip to Africa*, by 8-year-old Atlantis Tye Browder, they shared their narratives with their peers. While sharing, and listening to his peers' narratives, one student said he felt "stuck." His peers helped him find new ideas and inspiration to keep writing. Reading, writing about, and collectively responding to pro-Black, African-centric texts like this is part of the "intergenerational work of [culturally sustaining pedagogies of] imagining and enacting an education that . . . sustains life" (Paris, 2020, p. 373).

The teachers also sustain life during writing by urging children to write across and in the language they speak in and to tell the stories that they are comfortable with. One year, Alicia's students listened to the book, *Maybe Something Beautiful/Quizás Algo Hermoso* by F. Isabel Campoy, which is about how a group of kids made maps of their neighborhoods. Then her students created an "identity text" by drawing maps and labeling the beautiful things in their own neighborhoods and then writing about those places across languages. As they wrote, Alicia encouraged children to "do the best that they can" and to "listen for sounds and write the letters for those sounds," "write in Spanish or English or both." Roderick has learned from Alicia about ways to honor and extend children's languages and identities in writing. For example, at the start of a unit he created for Hispanic Heritage Month, called "Language is our Cultural Passport," children wrote down a list of heritage language expressions their parents, other adults, siblings, or others use at home when they are happy, proud, upset, excited, sad—like "Aye Dios mio!"/"Oh my God!" or "Give me some dap!" Kids were encouraged to use these expressions in their writing.

During independent writing, Kerry encourages children to listen for and write the first sound in a word, then the first and the last, and finally the first, middle, and last as they write. Usually by late winter in kindergarten, children can listen for and write as many sounds as they can hear. Roderick does the same, especially for writers who are not confident—he wants to build children's confidence as writers so they will always see themselves as authors. Sometimes children need the teachers' or other children's support to mediate this process of listening for and writing the sounds in words—teachers' and peers' speech becomes a sociocultural tool that helps them navigate the complex process of writing (Vygotsky, 1978).

Independent writing time starts out very short at the start of the year and grows longer over time, depending on the grade level and children's comfort and writing stamina. Next, the teachers confer with children one-on-one or work with a small group on a particular skill, strategy, or goal.

Conferring. It is common for children to need assistance when they are completing new tasks (Rogoff, 2003); conferring creates a space for that to happen. When conferring with children, the teachers usually start by asking open-ended questions like, "Tell me about what you're working on." The child then might read their work aloud. The teachers then tell children something they did well (like, "I noticed you wrote words in both Spanish and English! That helps explain things better than just using one language at a time." or "You labeled your drawings. That helps people know what is happening in your story!"). Then the teacher might suggest one thing the child can work on next.

In one goal-focused writing conference, Roderick asked a child "Why did you write some of the words in Spanish?" The child responded, "Mr. Peele, you told us to write how we say things when we are not in school because it is special to who we are. And my cousin and mom are talking in this story and they mostly speak Spanish!" Offering an air high five, Roderick said, "You are right!" Then, he asked the student about his writing goal—the child said, "make revisions."

Importantly, Alicia, Roderick, and Kerry foster *interdependence* by encouraging children to talk to one another about the questions and problems that come up during independent writing time. Before Kerry starts conferring with children, she has meetings with the class to talk about how to work together to solve typical problems that might come up. Kerry has also put on neon necklaces to concretely indicate that she is in a meeting and that children need to wait or ask a classmate for help. The teachers try to conference with each child once per week.

Alicia, Roderick, and Kerry try to keep the progression of multilingual writing, composing, and spelling development in mind as they confer with children; if they see children doing a particular thing well in their writing, they try to nudge them toward the next level. If the teachers notice that a few children all need support with a particular skill or are ready to try something new, then they might work with children in a group. For instance, in the fall of kindergarten, the majority of Kerry's class may be working on labeling their drawings, but a few children could also be writing sentences. If so, Kerry works on sentence-writing with a small group. Once she is ready to teach sentence-writing to the whole class, she can use a book one of those children made as an example. By using children's own writing in mini-lessons, she is critically centering and affirming their voices and languages.

During a writing conference, the teachers may also focus on helping kids remember spelling patterns and talking to kids about the different spelling patterns that different languages make. Kerry tells her students that because many children in her class speak different language varieties like African American Language (AAL); they may hear some letters and sounds in a different way. For example, in one conference, she talked to a student who heard /d/ instead of /th/ in the word "the." She told the child, "Sometimes the beginning of the word 'the' sounds like /d/ and sometimes it sounds like /th/." She and the other teachers discuss language patterns in this way because they don't want children to merely emulate Dominant English, but instead discuss and value multiple languages and language varieties through contrasting languages in ways that show the brilliance of being multilingual and multiliterate.

Revising and Editing. Revising and editing are approached carefully because the teachers want to provide feedback in ways that respect children's linguistic and cultural approximations. When teachers focus only on correcting "the basics" of a Dominant English norm in children's writing, they fall into advancing a "homogeneous view of language, in which it is a set of neutral rules; whatever the situation, those whose speech and writing follow the rules are proper, a cut above those who do not" (Dyson, 2013, p. 5). This is why Roderick's students set writing goals for each day of writing and for their in-process writing pieces overall. Setting personal goals creates purpose and a sense of ownership around the writing process. For example, after reading *Njinga of Ndongo and Matamba* by Ekiuwa Aire, another pro-Black, African-centric text that centers the lifeways of African communities, a child set a goal to revise by adding an ending to her personal narrative about a trip home to the Dominican Republic.

Alicia makes it a point to never write corrective feedback for revising or editing directly on children's writing. She writes notes, instructions, or corrections on sticky notes, which children use while they edit. She sometimes focuses on content over form, consistent with research on multilingualism (García, 2009). For example, Alicia read *The Best Part of Me* by Wendy Ewald, a nonfiction book that displays photos taken by children of their "best parts"; Alicia's students then took photos of their "best parts" and wrote about them. When a child wrote "The best part of me is my eyes. They are beauteful" Alicia did not correct the child's spelling of the word "beautiful" because it was early in the year and did not impact the writing's content (see Figure 6.1). Alicia's goal in providing feedback as children revise their writing is for children to find their voices, use their languages, and produce pieces that are appropriate for their writing abilities. She never wants children to think their writing is wrong, or that writing is laborious. As the year progresses, and children become more confident with their writing, Alicia may provide more corrective feedback or suggested revisions on sticky notes.

When Kerry provides feedback to children so that they can revise their writing, she might ask children to cross out the word. For instance, if the class had already studied the word "was," but one child was continuing to spell it as "wuz" during independent writing time, in a writing conference Kerry might remind the child about the conventional spelling for that word and help the child to add that spelling to the piece of writing (by asking the child to cross out "wuz" and write "was" in the space above) and also point them to the words on their word list. In providing this feedback, Kerry maintains a tone of kindness and care.

Share Time. In hybridized, culturally sustaining writing workshops, children are authors among other authors (Bakhtin, 1984). Share time is yet another space to respond to the ways children "author complex selves by responding to others in those spaces" (Dyson, 2013, p. 7). During share time, the children come together in the meeting area. The teachers might ask one child to share a whole piece of writing or part of it. They often share the work of a child who has tried very hard, taken a risk, or used the skill or strategy from the mini-lesson. This shows children how it might look to try out what they were taught and help them feel that they can do it, too. Having the opportunity to share work creates a space of "we," where children come to know that they are authors that have an audience (Souto-Manning & Yoon, 2018).

Writing Tools. Sociocultural theorists posit that cognitive processes and dominant social norms can be transformed through the use of cultural tools. (Rogoff, 2003; Vygotsky, 1978, 1997). In the hybridized, culturally sustaining writing workshop, sociocultural tools like writing utensils, paper, folders, notebooks, blank books, and paper—usually stored in a writing area or center—help ground the writing process. But it is really the social interactions around writing—the multimodal tools of multilingual speech and situated meaning-making among teachers and children and communities—that transforms and sustains the lifeways of communities (Dyson, 2013; Paris, 2020). Here are some physical tools children use:

- **Crayons:** For the first 6–8 weeks in kindergarten, children use crayons; then they transition to using pens and pencils so that children can focus on adding details and writing more pieces rather than on adding color. They add color to one book they have made that they would like to get ready to share with the class and put on a shelf in the classroom library.
- **Colored pencils:** Alicia finds children are very excited to write and draw with colored pencils!
- **Short golf pencils:** Because these pencils have no erasers, children do not get stuck on perfection and erasing but rather continue to write. If they make a mistake, they can cross out their mistake and write or draw what they meant to write/draw in a space nearby.
- **Felt-tipped pens:** These make a nice line and don't require too much hand pressure.
- **Pencil grips:** These rubber devices fit on a pencil to help children grip the pencil in a way that is comfortable.
- **Blank books:** Use three pages in kindergarten and the first part of 1st grade, then four pages. At first the pages are totally blank, then they have drawing boxes, and then more lines as kids' writing skills grow.
- **Writing folder:** These folders have a side for books the children are working on and a side for books they are done working on for now. Alphabet and high-frequency word charts are inserted into the middle of the folder, attached with prongs in the center, and are inside plastic sleeves.
- **Thinking notebooks/writer's notebooks:** In 2nd and 3rd grade, the teachers use writer's notebooks or journals.
- **Multimodal tools:** In 2nd and 3rd grade, students often use their iPad or personal computer to create texts.

Units. During the hybridized writing workshop, the teachers usually teach a series of thematic units focused on particular aspects of writing (see Table 6.3). These units usually correspond with the genres they are studying

Table 6.3. Writing Units

Kindergarten	1st–3rd Grade
Developing a Writerly Self/Identity Texts	**Writing Routines**
Units focused on feeling like a writer, and exploring our languages and communities through multimodal writing	Units focused on classroom procedures, using writing tools, and planning your writing
Writing Routines	**Developing a Writerly Self/Identity Texts**
Units focused on using writing tools and planning your story	Units focused on feeling like a writer and exploring our languages and communities through multimodal writing
First, Next, Last	
Units focused on drawing pictures in a sequence	
Labeling	**Making Work Easy to Read/Conventions**
Units focused on labeling drawings with first and/or first and last and/or first, middle, and last sound	Units focused on comparing and contrasting language forms and structures and using conventional language forms (e.g., spelling patterns)
List Books	**Personal Narrative**
Units that explore writing a book consisting of a title followed by drawings and words on every page that lists something about the title	Units focused on writing stories about personal and family experiences; can focus on characters and setting, problem and solution
Pattern Books	**All About Books**
Units that explore writing books, usually about one topic, that have a sentence with the same high-frequency word pattern on each page	Informational (nonfiction) writing units during which children research something and write "all about it"
	Realistic Fiction
How-to Books	Units that explore writing realistic (not fantasy) stories with characters, problems, and solutions
Units that explore writing books that explain procedures for activities	
Personal Narrative	**Poetry**
Stories about personal and family experiences	Units focused on writing poetry, usually connected to songs from children's lives, or an author study of a poet
Author Study	**Persuasive Writing**
Units that involve studying and writing books that replicate a particular author/illustrator's style (e.g., studying Donald Crews's books about transportation and writing similar books)	Units focused on making an argument and supporting that argument with evidence (e.g., letters to President Trump)

during the reading workshop. In that way, children have mentor-author models for the kind of writing they are doing. These units are fluid, though, and may change based on children's needs and current sociopolitical events (e.g., Alicia's class studied Amanda Gorman's inauguration poem *The Hill We Climb* when President Biden was elected).

In developing writing units, the teachers refer to different resources and experts in the field of early childhood writing instruction (e.g., Cleaveland, 2016; Horn & Giacobbe, 2007; Ray & Cleaveland, 2008; Ray & Glover, 2008; Ray, 2010; Seravallo, 2017; National Writing Project, 2022; Teachers College Reading and Writing Project, 2020). However, they never dictate the content of a child's writing within that unit. Choice is important as children develop agency and critical thinking skills to make their own choices in life. Through writing, the teachers want children to discover who they are and who they might become—and to speak to the issues that they care about. For example, when children in Alicia's class wrote letters to President Trump, they were not studying about writing persuasively or writing letters—they were working on personal narratives. Alicia knew students needed to write and just get all their feelings out. Once she gave them a chance to write in their writer's notebooks without interrupting them, she did a mini-lesson on the structure of a letter.

One year Roderick had a student who had a very difficult time finding himself in writing personal narratives. When Roderick later introduced a unit on poetry by having kids write "Where I'm From" poems, the boy connected the rhythms of poetry right away to his favorite rapper XXXTENTACION. Roderick asked how he learned about the rapper, and the student said it was from his older brother and explained how he connected to the songs when he was happy and sad. He produced several "Where I'm From" poems expressing how he felt about his brother. Later, Roderick encouraged him to write a personal narrative about him and his brother listening to rap. "Where I'm From" poetic activities were developed by George Ella Lyon, and you can learn more about them on their website: http://www.georgeellalyon.com/where.html.

Greenbelt Writing. The teachers usually have greenbelt writing for 1–2 weeks between units when they are reading in the next genre they will write in. Greenbelts are stretches of land—like Central Park or the large lawn stretching in front of Northern Parkway school—that provide people with spaces to enjoy trees, plants, grass, and nature. During these in-between periods, the teachers encourage children to use the time to cultivate their own topics and ideas.

Genre Study. The teachers study the different genres they are about to be writing about during reading workshop and interactive read-aloud time. For example, before they write realistic fiction, they read realistic fiction stories during read-aloud time and independent reading time to learn more about features of these books and can later incorporate them into books they make in that genre. During genre study, children can write a book or write about any topic and any genre.

When introducing a new writing genre, the teachers read aloud books in that genre that reflect many children's cultural and linguistic backgrounds and personal experiences. For instance, when studying personal narrative with kindergarteners, Kerry has read *Kitchen Dance* by Maurie J. Manning, which is about two children who wake up in the middle of the night and are excited to see their parents dancing in the kitchen. Characters in the story speak English and Spanish, like some students in Kerry's class.

When teachers are introducing a new genre of writing to the class, they also might work with the whole class to make a book in that genre. They make sure the class's book in this new genre is about a topic that is meaningful to children. One year, for example, when children were learning to make "how-to" books, or books that explain procedures for activities, Kerry decided their first class "how-to" book would be about how to make Dominican pastelitos, a type of pastry. She chose this topic because a student's parent had visited the classroom recently to teach children how to make cheese pastelitos. Many children were already familiar with pastelitos because they had eaten them with their families, as well. Having recently made pastelitos for their snack children were excited to make a book about them with Kerry, and they could describe the steps for creating them in detail. To make this class book, Kerry invited the children to share the steps they remembered with a partner in the meeting area. Then Kerry drew pictures and wrote their ideas on a few pieces of paper that were stapled together, like the books they would be using at writing time. Together, Kerry and the children thought of step 1, step 2, and step 3 for making these snacks. After children shared ideas for this class book, they each made their own book about how to make pastelitos during writing-workshop time, describing the steps in their own words. In the following days, children generated their own ideas for other how-to books as well, describing steps for how to play soccer, take care of a baby sister, and do other personally meaningful activities.

The teachers feel very fortunate to work at schools that allow them to create their own writing units in collaboration with the other teachers in their grade. However, if you don't have that freedom, think about small adjustments you can make to create spaces where writing can be a daily, generative, multilingual, creative, sustaining space.

Writing Celebrations. When children feel they have completed their book or piece of writing, then share time becomes a time to celebrate published writing. Inviting community input, the teachers may have a class celebration or livestream the celebration to invite families to hear and respond to children's work. These texts are often put on display on bulletin boards in and outside of the classroom. Figure 6.3 displays examples of published writing from Alicia, Roderick, and Kerry's classrooms.

Interactive and Group Writing

Children also engage in writing beyond the writing workshop. For example, children in Alicia and Roderick's classes often author the morning message. Children in all the classrooms are encouraged to write across their different languages and language varieties during choice time/work time or sometimes at the end of the day before the closing meeting or cipher. Children also write notes to each other and read each other's writing or during "Friendship Snack" (see Chapter 2). The teachers have also created group stories with children. To create a group story, children spend a little time each day dictating a story to the teachers, which can be made into class books that are placed in the classroom library. Interactive writing is another way to cultivate "we-ness" and reciprocal relationships grounded in children's cultures (Dyson, 2013). In this way, they respond to others as active agents rather than crafting standard language in isolation (Dyson, 2013). For example, when children in Alicia's class author the morning message, they write across their languages and read the message together. And when the class interactively writes words in the morning message, they work together to think about how to write a particular word or spelling pattern across linguistic codes.

Handwriting and Word Work

Alicia, Roderick, and Kerry also have brief designated daily times for handwriting and word work. Delpit (2012) asserts that teaching skills like these provides many children who have been marginalized by income, ethnicity, or language with the capital needed for success in schools. Alicia, Roderick, and Kerry know that children "not only need strong instruction in skills, but they need to know that it is skills, and not intelligence, that they lack" (Delpit, 2012, p. 57).

Handwriting. In the teachers' hybridized, culturally sustaining writing classrooms, handwriting instruction is framed around the importance of communication. For example, Roderick and his students initially talk about how the purpose of practicing handwriting is so they can write letters to their family. He explains to students that if they really want to tell people how they feel, people need to be able to read their handwriting." Since it is very common for children to write letters in reverse in any language, teaching handwriting is important (Bear et al., 2012; Graham et al., 2008). While there are debates about whether or not teachers should teach cursive

Figure 6.3. Published Writing in Three Classrooms

Mi Traditiones/My Traditions Quilts (2nd grade, Alicia)

First, Next, Last Drawings (Kindergarten, Kerry).

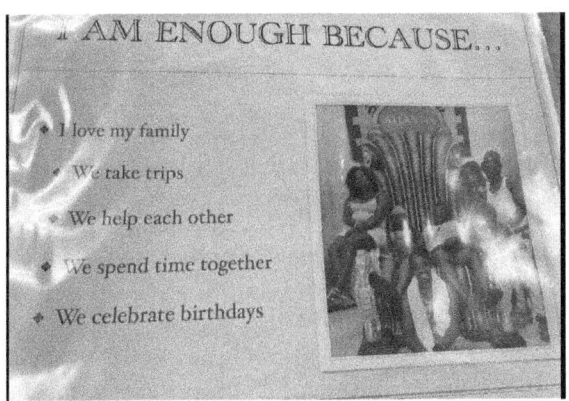

"I Am Enough" Book (3rd grade, Roderick)

or print handwriting, the research is pretty conclusive—teachers just need to teach some form of letter formation (Graham et al., 2008). Roderick and Alicia use their school's adopted curriculum to teach handwriting. All the teachers also take note of how children are gripping their pencils, and if they are gripping the pencil in their fists, they provide children with a "pencil grip," which is an ergonomic device that fits easily on a pencil and facilitates proper pencil holding. Kerry adapts her school's handwriting program, using the prompts the program suggests for showing and telling children how to write a letter ("big line down, little line across" for lowercase "t," for example). She also uses songs ("Always start your letters at the top"), and double-lined paper which has a midline and a bottom line, rather than paper that has a top line, a middle, dotted line, and a bottom line or one that has four lines (like the handwriting paper that Roderick and Alicia use). Kerry has found that the double-lined paper provides just the right amount of guidance for kids and is not confusing. When teaching handwriting, Kerry also describes categories of letters: letters are "small" (a, c, w, etc.), "tall" (t, k, f, etc.), or "hang below the bottom line" (g, j, y, etc.). Kerry teaches children lowercase letters first, following a letter-of-the-day approach, because many children are already familiar with writing capital letters and need more practice with lowercase letters.

The teachers try to make handwriting instruction authentic and integrated throughout the day. For instance, during other work times when children need to write letters, the teachers remind them of the letter formation and provide feedback about their formation. They want children to follow the formation so that they can write more efficiently, and they help keep children from reversing letters. For example, if they teach children to always form a "d" by writing a "little curve" first, children are more likely to write "d" with the correct formation. By contrast, if they started both "b" and "d" with a big line down, kids could get more confused and not remember which direction the curve should go in for "b" and "d." When teaching handwriting, the teachers often discuss the different ways letters and sounds are represented in different languages; as any hybridized, culturally sustaining teaching—even handwriting—celebrates "children's texts and utterances that integrate multiple languages, [language varieties], speech forms, and genres" (Machado, 2017, p. 311).

High-Frequency Words. The teachers foster knowledge of high-frequency words within purposeful writing activities. For learning high-frequency words, Alicia and Roderick give each child a book (a personal dictionary) containing a list of high-frequency words like those from Fry's list of 300. This book also contains blanks where children can write their own words. Then, children refer to their word lists or personal dictionaries as they write. Their word lists also contain self-generated, high-frequency words from their own lives and languages. In this way, a meaningful purpose for learning high-frequency words is framed. As Roderick says to his students, "We learn high-frequency words to better be able to share what we are thinking and how we are feeling with others!"

Kerry follows a process called orthographic mapping to help kids learn high-frequency words (Miles & Ehri, 2019). First, she tells children they are going to learn about a word in which the letters and sounds are doing things a little bit differently. First, they say the word and Kerry says it in a sentence; then she asks kids to suggest a sentence for that word. Then they count the sounds in the word, first with her modeling it and then with the kids doing so. Then they do the motions for the sounds. Then she asks kids to say the first sound and the letter. They keep going until they've spelled all the sounds in the word. Then they practice writing the word together on their whiteboards, saying the sounds in the word as they write. Doing orthographic mapping helps children remember the spelling for the word better than if she were to show them the whole word and ask them to memorize how it looks all at once (Miles & Ehri, 2019).

Dictation. The teachers also do word and sentence dictation with kids. They usually do this when they are learning decoding strategies in a small group. They practice writing words that Alicia or Kerry or Roderick say out loud with phonemic patterns they are learning at the time. For example, if they are learning about the /ch/ sound, they practice writing words with that sound, like "chat" and "lunch." Alicia might talk with children about the differences between that sound in Spanish (the "che") and in English. Dictation is not the same as a "spelling test." None of the teachers use spelling tests, as this decontextualized practice is not supported by research. Instead, they ask children to keep track of words they are excited about and they then learn the meanings of these words in context.

CONCLUSION

Culturally sustaining pedagogies recognize that "the purpose of state-sanctioned schooling has always been to forward the largely assimilationist and often violent white imperialist project" (Paris, 2020, p. 368). Culturally sustaining pedagogies pose the question "What spaces are we willing to relinquish, reshape, and reclaim to make necessary space for centering us and/or others, our lifeways and/or other lifeways in our spaces of teaching and learning?" (Paris, 2020, p. 368).

What if Alicia hadn't reshaped and reclaimed the writing workshop into an agentive, hybridized space where children could talk back to President Trump? Alicia recognized the necessity of pedagogies that help children divest from and reject white supremacist gazes and discourses that position Black, Indigenous, and migrant communities as disposable and damaged

(Paris, 2020). In writing, young children are newcomers with locally grounded ways of being, doing, and knowing writing. When teachers create hybridized routines and structures and provide multilingual, multimodal contexts and tools for writing, children can put those ways of being, doing, and knowing into practice. Then, writing can become a space to resist, to divest from, and to exclaim, as Alicia's student in her letter to President Trump—*you can't say my parents are bad or evil.*

CHAPTER 7

Attending to Children
Literacy Assessment That Cultivates Joy and Genius

*Kindel Turner Nash, Alicia Arce-Boardman,
Roderick Peele, and Kerry Elson*

One year, after looping with his students, Roderick informally assessed children's phonological awareness through a game adapted from the school phonics curriculum. He said "I want you to listen to and write the letter I say, without looking at me." Calling out "Write letter /B/!" "Write letter /T/," he noticed faces lighting up as children showcased genius and joy in their writing. He heard children exclaim, "I remember, I need to write it like this!" He saw children offer advice to friends, "Remember, hold your pencil this way, it will be easier."

Roderick's assessment story echoes Muhammad's (2020) guidance, "educators don't need to empower students or give them brilliance or genius . . . the power and genius is already within them" (p. x). It also illuminates Clay's (2013) words, "if we attend to individual children as they work . . . our detailed observations can lead us . . . to meet the learning needs of particular children in the formative stages of new learning" (p. 4).

In the pursuit of the inherent fullness—the joy and genius—of children, this book has presented practices and processes, grounded in current literacy research and a model and interpretive framework for culturally sustaining early literacy learning and teaching. Rooted in our North Star theories, we have showcased practices that strive to bridge children's ancestral and cognitive abilities as they exist in cultures, languages, and communities—this is what culturally sustaining pedagogies (CSPs) require. These practices necessitate large and small adjustments and mediations every hour, every day, every week, every month, and every year. Such adjustments are based on

> **Focus Question:** How can teachers use early literacy assessments to cultivate children's joy and genius?

observation and documentation of children over time to *attend to children,* to cultivate their joy and genius. These kinds of adjustments are at the heart of literacy assessment in the teachers' classes.

After presenting a definition of literacy assessment grounded in our theoretical perspectives, this chapter highlights: (1) everyday assessments, (2) concepts about print, (3) running records of oral reading fluency, (4) letter and sound naming, (5) vocabulary, and (6) spelling and phonemic awareness and then connects these to the features of CSPs. The assessments we discuss are typically called "inventories." Inventories are rooted in formative observations of children's language and literacy development (Afflerbach, 2017). The research, principles, and techniques we describe provide foundational knowledge to assess children in authentic, contextualized, culturally sustaining ways.

Many assessments we describe are grounded in Clay's extensive research on early literacy assessment (Clay, 1982, 1991, 2001, 2010, 2013) and her Observation Survey of Early Literacy Achievement (2013). We also draw on other current research accounting for the richness of languages and cultures and the importance of accounting for cultural and linguistic bias in early language and literacy assessment practices (Bear et al., 2012; Briceño & Klein, 2019; Dutro, 2010; Dyson, 2013; Genishi & Dyson, 2009; Nash & Piña, 2020; Noguerón-Liu, 2020; Wheeler et al., 2012; Yoon, 2015).

A WORD ABOUT STANDARDIZED AND HIGH-STAKES ASSESSMENTS

The idea of assessment as observations of children and adjustments to practice in pursuit of joy and genius may run contrary to what you have heard about literacy "assessment." We live in an age of accountability—"assessment" has been conflated with high-stakes and standardized assessments. Yet standardized assessments can (and often do) act as a tool for sorting by predetermined standards, ideologies, and broad generalizations of a norm (Genishi & Dyson, 2009; Yoon, 2015). Further, many standardized assessments are culturally and linguistically biased (Laing & Kamhi, 2003) and tell us little about children and what they need to know (Clay, 2013).

In early childhood, accountability-based assessments are often based on the idea of "readiness." Readiness is "a social construct that is determined by cultural norms that are upheld by those in power" (Yoon, 2015, p. 368). While learning is multifaceted and hyperbolic, readiness "demands that children grasp a defined skills set, deemed rigorous, with timely developmental progressions" (Yoon, 2015, p. 368). High-stakes assessments and the urgency of "readiness" narrow instruction, curricula, and reduce time spent reading and writing (Berliner, 2011; Dutro, 2010). Yoon's (2015) study of high-stakes assessment practices in an urban school found that standardized assessments are *taking over* teacher collaboration, instructional time, and authentic interaction and discussion about observations of children.

Time becomes compressed and surveilled—"panoptical time"—oriented toward scripted skills and test scores (Genishi & Dyson, 2009, p. 111). Deep cultural analysis becomes difficult with constricted standardized measures (Pollock, 2008).

High-stakes assessments are often used in response to intervention (RTI), a widely used process which focuses on tiered skills-based interventions. RTI is frequently used as a standard treatment protocol involving screening, diagnosis, progress monitoring, and outcome assessments (Lipson et al., 2011). Children's scores are placed on data walls that sort children into categories (Yoon, 2015). Standardized assessments may be publicly aimed at reducing "achievement gaps," but instead they invoke colormuteness about race, a racism-without-racists (Bonilla-Silva, 2017; Pollock, 2009). Noguera and Alicea (2020) argue that this is the result of structural racism that is baked into all schools, but into urban and other marginalized and underfunded schools in particular. Afflerbach (2017) details a problem-solving approach to RTI, which allows and encourages input from observational and reading inventories. In the problem-solving approach, the "data wall" portraying standardized data results serves as a discussion starter to talk about what a child knows, what social and emotional needs a child might have, and what deep observations teachers have made about a child.

Although Alicia, Roderick, and Kerry and their students are subject to discourses and practices of high-stakes, standardized assessments, observations of children over time are the most essential assessments for cultivating students' joy and genius.

Defining Assessment: A Process to Help Children Learn More

Genishi and Dyson (2009) define assessment as "an ongoing, complex process in which we aim to discover and document what children are learning over time in many situations and across multiple symbol systems, so that we can help them learn more" (p. 116). We adopt this definition because it is rooted in the way we view and define literacy as the ability to read, write, visualize, listen, and talk about multiple kinds of texts. The way people read, write, visualize, listen, and talk is socially, culturally, linguistically, and historically situated within disciplines, contexts, structural inequities, and systems of oppression. As such, literacy assessment that is culturally sustaining is embedded in practices of developing deep knowledge and understanding of children and their communities and observing children's literacy work over time. It is a process that helps teachers learn more.

The Purpose of Assessment and Seven Overarching Principles

Alicia notes how relationships are essential in order to be able to assess children. Through practices embedded in communal love and trust, children talk to one another and answer questions and share about their lives, languages, and cultures. Drawing on these relationships, the teachers can then utilize formative (providing ongoing feedback) and summative (evaluating mastery of objectives) assessments to understand what skills and knowledge children have and what they need to learn.

Seven overarching principles guide the way the teachers document children's learning over time: (1) Never be punitive. (2) Support children's learning pursuits. (3) View assessment as a piece, not the puzzle itself. (4) Understand that standardized assessments are not measures of intelligence and are often biased. (5) Never allow assessments to make children feel pressured and stressed. (6) Use assessment to provide specific and useful feedback to children. (7) Conduct assessments in authentic contexts. Thus, the purpose of assessments is to help teachers gain clarity about children's learning pursuits of skills, identity, intellect, and criticality (Muhammad, 2020). Assessments guide how Alicia, Roderick, and Kerry teach and help them to understand what skills and knowledge children already have and what they need to learn—that is how they can ensure that their instruction is culturally sustaining.

These seven principles push against racist, reductive frameworks that are based in shallow understandings of culture (Gutiérrez & Johnson, 2017). At the center of their work as teachers are their *everyday assessments* grounded in astute observations.

Everyday Assessments

Alicia, Roderick, and Kerry live by their everyday assessments. They utilize these assessments to provide feedback in what Roderick calls strengths-based check-ins. Essential everyday assessments include:

- **Note-taking and Conferences:** The teachers use informal observational or anecdotal notes during their conferences with children. Kerry and Roderick use a note-taking sheet on 8½" × 11" paper, with a box for each child's name and a space to record notes; Alicia uses a checklist with each child's name and each subject area. The teachers try to visit each child for a conference at least once a week, and they work more frequently with children who need more support. The teachers note what they talked about in the box, not only to help them remember what the child was working on, but also to keep track of whom they have visited and who still needs a visit or conference. As noted in Chapter 4, conferences can focus on any number of reading strategies, but often focus on using and assessing children's use of important comprehension strategies (visualizing, inferring, asking and answering questions, etc.).
- **Planning Notes:** In the past, during small groups, the teachers have written plans on a planning sheet and then written notes on what they observed each child doing during the group. For example, if

a lot of kids in the group didn't know a particular high-frequency word that they were working on, then they would note that and make sure to review that word with kids next time they met with them.
- **Photos:** Alicia, Roderick, and Kerry take photos to help document the curriculum for themselves and for families. They may look at photos to recall the types of work kids have done during workshop or work time or to recall information about their social interactions when they are writing summative reports. They might look at photos to remember times when a child showed leadership skills. The photos have also helped teachers see how long a child may have worked on a project. They try to take photos of kids' work over time; seeing these photos can help with showing growth over time and can also foster a sense of the child's stamina and persistence. The teachers mostly use information from photos for portfolios, newsletters, and formal reports for families.
- **Checklists:** Alicia, Roderick, and Kerry use checklists and charts as assessment tools in a variety of ways. In the past, Kerry has also filled out a sheet during work time that helps her know where everyone went for that day. It's a grid, and it has each child's name going down vertically and many boxes next to each child's name. She writes the date at the top of the grid; then, moving vertically, she'll note where that child spent the most time at work time. For example, she'd write "BL" for blocks and "PT" for painting. Keeping track of where the child goes during work time helps Kerry know the child more as well, and the more she knows about children, the more connected she feels to them. Knowing what they like to do basically continues to help her understand them as people. She can also use the information to develop a curriculum. For instance, sometimes she notices that children make scraps of paper at the paper table into little creatures that move around, so when that happens, she sometimes introduces the idea of making puppet shows if they haven't tried doing that on their own. Alicia and Roderick make checklists for children to use. For example, if a child needs to work on remembering to add a certain type of punctuation, they will make a checklist that children can use each time they finish with their writing.

These forms of everyday assessment connect to CSPs' focus on critically centering languages and drawing on student and community agency and input. Everyday assessments as described allow the teachers to construct deep understandings of children's literacies and languages in order to critically center these in their teaching. Since these forms of assessment involve sitting alongside children and observing, listening, and hearing them, they naturally foster student input as a valued and central part of their planning, teaching, and learning processes.

Concepts of Print

As young children interact with the written word all around them—in advertisements on television and YouTube videos, while texting their auntie from their tablet, on the McDonald's sign on the way home from school, and on books, mail, cereal boxes, big box stores, and more—they develop Concepts about Print (CAP). Linked to cognitive theory, CAP are the features of written words, the way print moves directionally; the letters, and letter patterns (e.g., digraphs, consonant blends) that make sounds to form words and sentences and paragraphs and books; the punctuation marks that convey emotions, tell where sentences end, or tell when people are talking; and the sequence of where books begin and end. Nearly a half century of research shows that children learn CAP quickly when they engage in literacy activities *at school* (Clay, 2013; Owocki & Goodman, 2002). Assessing children's CAP tells us what children are recognizing and thinking about the print around them. When they begin to point to words and ask, "What does that mean?" they indicate that they know that print means something—and this is very important information that can guide children to learn more (Owocki & Goodman, 2002). Assessing CAP at the pre-K/kindergarten/1st-grade level reveals clues to support children along their literacy journeys. CAP assessments include Clay's (2013) CAP observation task. That task uses specific books that Clay has authored. If you do not have access to these books, there are other widely available CAP tools, like the Teachers College Reading and Writing Project CAP abbreviated or full 13-point assessment, which Kerry's school uses (https://readingandwritingproject.org/resources/foundational-skills-assessments).

In order to move toward being CSP-oriented, any CAP assessment should be conducted in the context of reading an actual, culturally and linguistically authentic book with an individual child. Previous chapters have described the ways in which the teachers select culturally and linguistically authentic books by choosing books about Black, Indigenous, and Other People of Color that are written and illustrated by group members (and/or are bilingual) and are focused on everyday experiences (Boutte, 2002). This kind of reading material contributes to making CAP assessment CSP-oriented because children identify with the story and language, and can make connections based on their culturally and linguistically constructed experiences.

Letter and Sound Naming

As noted elsewhere in the book, there are 26 uppercase and lowercase letters in the English alphabet, but there are 42–44 speech sounds, including about 20 vowel phonemes and only 6 vowels (Share, 2008). This is why it can take children multiple years to learn to read in English, as compared to only 1 year for those learning to read languages with a more transparent orthographic system (Seymour et al., 2003). Although they are concerned about a reinvigorated emphasis on bottom-up, analytical, rigid approaches to teaching alphabetic, phonemic, and phonological awareness, the teachers do feel that it is important to understand which letters and sounds children understand. A letter-identification assessment helps the teachers understand how children are attending to the symbols of the alphabet. Additionally, a letter–sound correspondence assessment can help the teachers understand how children are associating sounds with letters. As with the concepts about print assessment, this task is necessary only if a child does not know all of the letters. This task can be given in multiple languages and across multiple alphabetic systems so that teachers can contrastively analyze children's languages and base their teaching on what children know about the alphabet(s) and sounds.

Clay's (2013) observation task for letter identification assesses all letters, both lowercase and uppercase. When assessing children, the letters should be treated in random fashion, not in alphabetical order. A letter name, a sound, or a word beginning with the letter are acceptable responses, because these tell us that the child knows the letter in some way. Procedures for this task are simple, and the assessment should take 5–10 minutes. The teacher prepares a letter card or sheet and introduces the assessment task by saying, "What do you call these? Can you find some that you know?" Then the teacher points to the letters horizontally left to right. If a child is hesitant, Clay (2013) recommends beginning with the first letter of the child's name. A masking card can be used if necessary. A separate scoring sheet should be used. This task can also be used as a letter–sound correspondence assessment—Save it for another day, though! Other letter naming as well as letter–sound correspondence assessments are widely available online (e.g., https://readingandwritingproject.org/resources/foundational-skills-assessments). If children are multilingual or have multiple language varieties, approximations of letters that are related to language should be counted as correct (Briceño & Klein, 2019; Wheeler et al., 2012).

It can be important to know what letters, and perhaps sounds, children understand to inform teaching of decoding strategies, but letter naming is a limited way of telling us what children know about letters (Clay, 2013). For example, Yoon (2013) found that kindergarten children at an urban school who "failed" the letter-naming assessment repeatedly identified and playfully discussed the letters of one another's table name tags during writing time. The implications of this study are that assessments need to be contextualized within real and social language and literacy practices and activities. Thus, using letter-naming assessments in ways that are culturally sustaining, teachers try to conduct these assessments in the context of children's real reading, writing, and talking. In that way, children and their multiple ways of being, knowing, and doing are at the center of the letter-naming assessment.

Running Records

Often in schools, young children's reading ability is measured only by what letters, sounds, and words they know. However, running records provide information about how children are applying that phonological and morphological knowledge to actual reading. As noted in Chapter 4, a running record is a way of understanding and documenting a child's oral reading fluency and comprehension. Running records are a type of oral reading or informal reading inventory, an assessment that uses observations and standard notations or codes to document reading behaviors (Rodgers et al., 2021).

Running records draw from a sociocultural theoretical perspective and from the research of Marie Clay (2013) and that of Goodman et al. (1987), which suggests that there are three "cueing systems" that children utilize as they read: meaning (semantics), language structure (syntax), and visual (graphophonics). The most widely used running record in U.S. schools is that of Fountas and Pinnell (2016). This is the type of running record used by Alicia, Roderick, and Kerry's schools; however, they all take frequent running records as noted below in between the benchmark assessments, which are typically only done at the beginning, middle, and end of the year.

To take a running record, the teacher listens to a child read a text of 100–200 words for at least 1 minute, marking every word read accurately with a tick or checkmark on a recording sheet or a blank piece of paper. The teacher typically takes running records during a reading conference or when other children are working independently. Clay (2013) recommends choosing texts that teachers feel are at a child's independent, instructional, and frustration levels. Many texts can be leveled using scholasticbookwizard.com or another online or lexile leveling system. While the child reads, the teacher records the child's errors or miscues. The miscues that children make include substitutions, omissions, insertions, and repetitions. The teacher also makes note of when children self-correct, when they appeal to the teacher for a word, and when they are told the word (see Figure 7.1).

Culturally authentic texts that the child will be interested in are more appropriate than preprinted, disconnected passages or texts (Clay, 2013). This is because many preprinted and standardized assessments are situated in White, middle-class values and modes of communication (Yoon, 2015).

Children Who Speak Language Varieties and/or Are Multilingual. For multilingual language speakers and children who have language varieties, accuracy in English reading should not be the single goal, and at times it is not even an appropriate one. Instead, while maintaining high expectations, teachers should focus on *content* over the *form* of language (Alvarez, 2012). If running records are collected, Briceño and Klein's (2019) research with multilingual children determined a need for teachers to distinguish between language-related errors and what they call "language approximations." These approximations are attributable to a reader's language. For example, if a multilingual

Attending to Children

Figure 7.1. Running Records

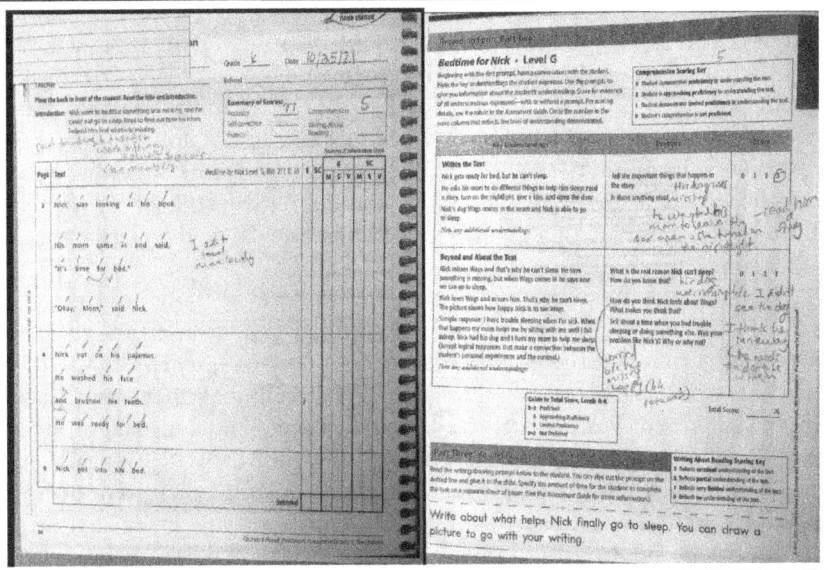

child reads "he say" instead of "he said," this indicates that the child understands the meaning of the word said, but may not have learned the past tense of the verb "say" yet. This error is different from an error in misinterpreting the visual cues from the printed text (Briceño & Klein, 2019, p. 613). Similarly, Wheeler and colleagues (2012) note that teachers should consider language approximations of speakers of African American Language (AAL). For example, if an AAL speaker reads "he say" instead of "he said," that indicates that the child is applying a phonological feature of AAL, simplifying when possible (see Figure 4.1). By accounting for the role played by students' cultures, languages, and language varieties during reading, Alicia, Roderick, and Kerry can then ground and expand their instruction in ways that are culturally and linguistically sustaining.

Scoring and Interpreting Running Records. To score running records with Dominant English–speaking children, teachers should count the number of words read accurately and subtract that number from the total number of words. If a child can read a passage of text with 95–100% accuracy, then the text is considered to be at their independent level. Between 90–94%, texts are at an instructional level, and at 80–89% and below texts are at a child's frustration level (Clay, 2013). Conversion charts for scoring are available in Clay's books (2013), and some conversion calculators that help determine the error and self-correction ratios can be found online (e.g., https://www.wordcalc.com/runningrecord/). The standard is that 10 errors out of 100 would equal 90% accuracy (Rodgers et al., 2021).

For Alicia, Roderick, and Kerry, scoring the running record quantitatively is only the first step; interpreting the running record is a key level of analysis that helps them understand what information the reader is attending to and what information they are neglecting. They look at each error, asking themselves "Why did the child do that?" Did the meaning influence the error? Did the sentence structure or a word in the sentence influence the child? Did visual information from the text influence the error? Meaning-related errors tell teachers about how a child is making sense of the text; is the error related to the child looking at the rest of the sentence, or the pictures, or the background?"

For example, does the child read "girl" instead of "lady" or "man" instead of "boy?" In this case, the child inferred the meaning of the text—perhaps by looking at the picture, instead of the letters, when the word was tricky. Syntax is the structure of language. If a child makes an error that relates to sentence or word structure, such as reading "lake" instead of "lady," then we see that they are looking at the structure of words as they read. Visual errors have to do with the way letters, words, or clusters of letters look. Reading the word "lake" for "lady" is also a visual error. It shows us how the visual information influenced the way the child read the word. If a child reads "bil" for "bicycle," this is a purely visual error. At this point, teachers make and circle their notations about the specific type of errors and/or self-corrections the child makes while reading—meaning, syntax, and visual (MSV) (Clay, 2013).

It is crucial that teachers take their knowledge of children's cultures, languages, and language varieties into account when scoring and interpreting running records. For multilingual children who are learning English as another language, after analyzing the running records for errors, they reanalyze, looking at all of the "tolds," or words that the teacher provided for the child, verb tense, contractions, prepositions, plural -s approximations, and other language-related approximations to make note of the impact on the overall meaning, sources of information drawn on or neglected, and other comments. Multilingual children's approximations should not be counted as an automatic error; instead teachers count all errors of the same type as one error. When conducting running records with speakers of AAL, the research suggests that teachers should make two calculations, one including all errors and another excluding all language approximations related to AAL (Briceño & Klein, 2019; Wheeler et al., 2012). The calculations should not be used punitively (remember our principles!), rather they should be used as a way to understand and help children and teachers compare the differences between AAL and Dominant English. The protocol is different for these children because it allows teachers to create a more accurate portrait of their actual language abilities.

When used in ways that don't try to erase children's languages (and, by extension, cultures), running records help guide teaching, assess how challenging a text is for a child, and show progress over time—so that teachers can learn more. As noted in Chapter 4, especially for children in 2nd and 3rd grade, most recent research suggests that running records should *not* be used for ability grouping. Instead, they should be used the way Alicia, Roderick, and Kerry use them—to help guide their instructional choices toward culturally sustaining teaching.

VOCABULARY

Assessing vocabulary knowledge can be complicated because there are multiple types of vocabulary—high-frequency and sight-word vocabulary and conceptual receptive and expressive vocabulary (Stahl et al., 2019). Further, vocabulary varies by cultural and linguistic membership—there is no right or standardized set of vocabulary. Thus, we discuss examples of authentic vocabulary assessments in each area.

High-Frequency Word Reading. To assess high-frequency words, many use Fry's (1980) high-frequency English words (e.g., https://www.k12reader.com/subject/vocabulary/fry-words/) or other word lists like Clay's (2013) word-reading task. Similar to letter/sound naming assessments, high-frequency words can be printed on a sheet or card (or index cards) while teachers use a separate scoring sheet to mark the words the child knows. This quick assessment can also be conducted in authentic contexts over time. For example, Kerry analyzes children's writing or reads with children and asks them to identify words. Word-reading assessments should be conducted multiple times a year. The words on Fry's list are only a starting point for the teachers. They find that children need to work on other high-frequency words, such as the names of their friends or family members, often in the context of writing. That is why Alicia Roderick and Kerry may include these words on lists that children use when writing.

Authentic Vocabulary Assessments. Standardized vocabulary assessments are often linguistically and culturally biased (Laing & Kamhi, 2003). Further, most measure only receptive vocabulary (Pearson et al., 2007). Contextualized vocabulary checklists, on the other hand, are simple tables that show target vocabulary words being assessed, with a space for teachers to check whether children understand and use the word in the context of instruction. These checklists can assess the children's comprehension of 10–15 weekly vocabulary words. Figure 7.2 shows a checklist that Alicia created to assess children's bilingual vocabulary knowledge in a unit about activists under 30, grounded in the text set *I Know My Bill of Rights* by Mysonne Linen and Heddrick McBride, *You Are Mighty: A Guide to Changing the World* by Caroline Paul, and *Oh the Things That We're For* by Innosanto Nogaro.

Beyond charts and checklists, the teachers assess vocabulary in everyday ways by listening, observing, and analyzing assignments. In Roderick's

Figure 7.2. Vocabulary Checklist

distraught/*inquietísimo*	✓✓
discrimination/*discriminacion*	✓✓
daunting/*desalentador/dora*	✓
encouragement/*el ánimo*	✓

classroom, vocabulary books and a graffiti wall (word wall) document children's expressive vocabulary knowledge. As children document new words and place them in their vocabulary books and on the word wall, Roderick notices children use their newfound vocabulary words throughout the day. These kinds of vocabulary assessments are culturally sustaining because they occur within the context of instruction that is connected and historicized within the languages, cultures, and neighborhoods their students inhabit.

Writing Vocabulary Task. The Writing Vocabulary task (Clay, 2013) is a useful assessment for understanding early vocabulary, language use, quality, and directionality in prekindergarten and kindergarten children. This 10-minute (at the most) assessment asks children to write their own name, as well as "all the words you know how to write." Children can be prompted during this assessment if they need help. For example, a teacher might say "Can you write the word *go*"? If a children say they cannot write their name, they can be prompted to write single- and two-letter words: "Do you know how to write *is*? (pause) *to*? (pause) *I*?" This open-ended assessment is rooted in what children know and can do, rather than in a predetermined set of items that measures one child against another.

SPELLING AND PHONEMIC AWARENESS

In order for Alicia, Roderick, and Kerry to know which words and word parts to study, they need an idea of children's emergent spelling. In addition to the spelling inventories described below, the teachers often find that observing children's writing periodically gives them valuable information about their spelling growth.

Spelling Inventories. In Kerry's 1st-grade class, a primary spelling inventory (PSI) is used. The PSI, used to assess children's initial knowledge of spelling patterns, is recommended for K–3rd grade (Bear et al., 2012). Chapter 6 noted the fluid stages of spelling. The PSI assessment builds from knowledge about those fluid stages. The PSI contains 26 simple consonant–vowel–consonant (CVC) words, digraphs, and blends and words with inflectional endings (-ed, -ing). For kindergarten and other emergent readers, Kerry only assesses children's attempts at spelling the first five words. For beginning readers, she assesses their attempts at spelling the first 15 words. With more advanced spellers, she uses the entire list. This inventory is administered like a spelling test (but we don't condone spelling tests!). Children are given a numbered paper and they "spell the best they can" as the teacher dictates each word. A feature guide is used to analyze children's errors and confirm a child's approximate (and fluid) stage of spelling (Bear et al., 2012). Spelling inventories and feature guides are included in the *Words Their Way* series (Bear et. al., 2012) and are also available through many online sources.

Children Who Speak Language Varieties and/or Are Multilingual. Multilingual children and those who speak language varieties bring what they know about sounds and spelling from their heritage language as they learn English. For example, Spanish learners may find it difficult to spell words that are difficult to differentiate in their heritage language. In one study, Spanish speakers made substitutions between complex contrasts such as /ch/ and /sh/ because there are no differences between these sounds in Spanish (Helman & Bear, 2007).

Thus, it is essential for teachers to observe children's heritage languages to better understand their biliteracy development. As you read in the section on running records, when children's spelling attempts reflect their heritage languages, teachers should use this information to contrastively teach the differences between the languages. Further, when children are learning a new language, teachers should not focus too much on language form over rich content.

Hearing and Recording Sounds in Words. As noted, as in many schools, Alicia, Roderick, and Kerry already have predetermined phonemic and phonological awareness assessments that are part of the curricula their schools use. There are many informal assessments that can help teachers learn about the way children are becoming attuned to syllables or the phonological units of words (phonological awareness) and phonemic awareness (isolating, categorizing, and blending phonemes, onsets, and rimes). One example is the Test of Phonological Awareness (McKenna & Stahl, 2015), which measures children's understanding of rhymes, phoneme isolation, identification, and categorization. Standardized phonological and phonemic awareness assessments like Dynamic Indicators of Basic Early Literacy Skills (DIBELS), Achievement Improvement Monitoring System (AIMSweb), and Phonological Awareness Literacy Screening (PALS) are common in schools.

The Hearing and Recording Sounds in Words (Clay, 2013) is a simple tool to learn about children's phonemic awareness and spelling development—how children represent sounds (phonemes) with letters (graphemes). This dictation task involves the teacher in dictating a sentence and asking the child to write what they hear. The child is given credit for every phoneme even if the word is not spelled correctly. This task gives the teacher an idea of how children analyze words they hear and find ways to use letters to stand for the sounds they hear. This task also provides information about the child's use of capital letters, reversals, and sentence structure. This task is available as part of the Observation Survey of Early Literacy Assessment (Clay, 2013).

As with the other early literacy assessments described in this chapter, when implemented in the context of students' complex languages, histories, and experiences, assessments can provide useful input from students about what they *know* to inform culturally sustaining instruction that centers on children's and communities lifeways, ways of reading, and ways of writing.

CONCLUSION

Early literacy assessments can attend to and help teachers learn more about the language and literacy genius and fullness of children. The assessments described above help Alicia, Roderick, and Kerry implement effective and sustaining teaching practices through detailed documentation and observations about how children work over time—documentation and observation that accounts for children's cultures through contextualization and the use of texts that reflect children's heritage language and cultural knowledge. In contrast, standardized tests often label, pathologize, and amplify deficit rhetoric about the literacies, languages, and cultures of Black, Brown, Indigenous, and Other People Of Color and those who are poor (Dutro, 2010). We wonder, what if we spotlighted the genius—the brilliance, skills, intelligence, and creativity—flowing through children's communities for ages through early literacy assessment? What if we used assessment, as Roderick did, to cultivate the genius that is already there?

CHAPTER 8

An Epilogue
The Truth That's Already There

*Kindel Turner Nash, Alicia Arce-Boardman, Roderick Peele,
and Kerry Elson with Haydée Dohrn-Melendez Morgan*

> what really matters anyway?
> that i would observe the decay
> and decadence around me
> i mean the
> degeneration of our world
> flowing like a waterfall
> out of the mouths of scholars
>
> scholars who say
> kids who don't learn
> so many words by pre-k
> are doomed to fail in school
> something so wrong
> i can feel it in my bones . . .
> the money flows
> to those who will spout out
> "research" about
> "those disadvantaged kids" . . .
>
> what really matters,
> is the truth
> that's already there.
>
> (Nash, 2016, p. 11)

In 2014, a prestigious scholar came to Kindel's university as a keynote speaker for an annual urban education lecture series. You can imagine how thrilled Kindel felt—a junior scholar in her second year as an assistant professor—to have the chance to interact with this well-known scholar. At a forum for faculty and graduate students preceding the lecture, the scholar cited the word or language gap study, asserting that "urban" students need rich curricula because their parents don't talk at home. Although that study's findings have been debunked and its methodology found to be flawed (Dyson, 2015; Kuchirko, 2019; Tamis-LeMonda et al., 2017; Wasik et al., 2016), this prominent researcher was reifying racist and deficit notions about families in urban spaces.

It was this moment, along with the guidance of wise elders to understand the literacy practices that are already working in urban schools, that led Kindel into the racially, culturally, ethnically, and linguistically diverse classrooms of Alicia, Haydée, Kerry, and later Roderick to bring light to that truth. Kindel wrote the opening poem, and now with Alicia, Roderick, Haydée, and Kerry, this book to describe *the truth that's already there*—the already-existing genius within Communities of Color.

Paris and Alim (2017b) identify features of culturally sustaining pedagogies (CSPs) in practice. Throughout this volume, we have shared literature and connected examples of how we see these features in fluid motion within school communities and in the teachers' classrooms. Table 8.1 offers a summary of the features of CSP and examples.

Table 8.1. Summary of Culturally Sustaining Pedagogies Features from Chapters 2–7

Features of CSP	CSP Features in Action
1. Critically centering children's literacies, languages, and knowledge	Communicating with families in their heritage languages in and out of school
	Creating class meeting areas as third spaces that foster knowingness, belongingness, and agency
	Building class libraries that foster racial and linguistic justice
	Nurturing collaborative, collective, critical, and loving environments to support dynamic cultural identities
	Creating critical spaces through interactive read alouds
	Translanguaging and code-meshing in everyday talk and through creating "identity texts" (e.g., Class Books, Family Collages, Name Stories, I Am Webs)
	Centering languages in word work
	Fostering expressive and receptive language development through comparing, hybridizing, and meshing languages across linguistic and cultural repertoires
	Instructing in multifaceted, multilingual vocabulary through interactive read-alouds, play, word/graffiti walls and sorts, reader's theater, and interactive vocabulary study
	Hybridizing the reading and writing workshop (making own books, reading and writing across languages, dynamically grouping children)

Table 8.1. *(continued)*

Features of CSP	CSP Features in Action
2. Valuing children's and communities' agency and input so that we are accountable to the communities we serve	Fostering ecological community input through family playground gatherings, home and community visits, gathering of stories, and communication practices
	Creating rules and routines with children
	Forefronting family language and cultural traditions in classroom practices, routines, celebrations
	Centering student voices in morning meeting, share time, and closing cipher
	Using contrastive analysis to talk about languages, the alphabet, and words
	Engaging students' everyday talk and critical questions as curriculum
	Providing time to read across languages and cultures
	Centering children and family voices in the reading and writing workshop (e.g., choice writing, writing across languages, sharing writing with families)
	Creating multimodal texts (e.g., Flipgrid, 3-D books, The Best Part of Me)
	Centering children, not outcomes, in assessment
3. Historicizing content and instruction to connect learning to the histories of racial, ethnic, and linguistic communities, neighborhoods and cities, and the larger states and nation-states	Ensuring that classroom areas, libraries, and routines connect to children's and communities' histories and realities
	Establishing *confianza*, or mutual trusting relationships, to build an interdependent classroom community
	Using culturally rooted music in daily routines and instruction (e.g., during morning meetings, transitions, and author studies)
	Pushing back against bottom-up practices that normalize Dominant English (e.g., scripted phonics, isolated skills instruction)
	Engaging children's ways of knowing, being, and doing in reading and writing instruction (e.g., writing about bilingualism, family traditions, and personal narratives in heritage languages and varieties)
	Culturally mediating independent and guiding reading with high-level, high-interest, and multilingual texts
	Centering joy through life-affirming, antiracist and pro-Black read-alouds and spaces to read, talk, write, and think about these books
	Supporting language hybridity through daily greetings, talking, and singing
	Centering children's musical cultural traditions and love for dance by dancing and listening to music throughout the day
	Creating playful sites (choice time, games, Lego cities, hand claps) for oral language development
	Conducting contextualized assessments to learn more
	Valuing multilingual/language-variety speakers' language approximations in assessments
	Using culturally and linguistically authentic assessments

(continued)

Table 8.1. *(continued)*

Features of CSP	CSP Features in Action
4. Building children's and our own capacity to contend with internalized oppressions and to counter messages and systems that suggest that marginalized students and their families are the problem and value White, middle-class, monolingual, monocultural values	Creating conflict resolution routines like the cipher, friendship snack, and kindness meetings that foster kindness as justice Leaning in to and confronting sociopolitical realities like police brutality, colorism, xenophobia, linguicism and racism through literacy practices (e.g., identity maps, Black and Brown are Rainbow Colors, letter writing) Agentically engaging children in reading and writing against oppression (e.g., writing letters to Trump) Approaching oral language and vocabulary instruction in raciolinguistic, heteroglossic ways Pushing back against standardized practices and assessments focused on readiness by redefining assessment as observation and carefully documenting over time
5. Working with children and communities to sustain right, reciprocal relationships with the land	Learning about and acknowledging the Indigenous origins of the land and water of the region Learning about Indigenous movements to reclaim colonized lands and water (#NoDAPL) Writing persuasive essays about why or why not Columbus Day should or should not be a federal holiday Moving beyond traditional, whitewashed narratives of the Thanksgiving story
6. Curricularizing these features in learning settings	Examples of curricularizing features 1–5 are included above.

MISSTEPS AND TENSIONS

In sharing this book, we want to be clear that none of us have "arrived" at being culturally sustaining early literacy practitioners. We can only consciously and consistently work to move toward it. Paris and Alim (2017a) remind us that these features of CSPs are ambitious goals for them, even as the originators of these important and transformative ideas and concepts.

Throughout the multiyear research project that informed this book, the teachers and Kindel experienced so many missteps, tensions, and even failures. For example, one December, Alicia decided to bring an "elf on the

An Epilogue

shelf" into her classroom—like many teachers at her school were doing, and like she was doing at home. When she introduced the elf, inviting children to write a class story about it, the children in her class were perplexed. They stared blankly at her as she showed them the elf. Some had never seen an elf on the shelf, and few had one at home. One girl started crying (it does look a bit creepy!) Alicia took the elf back home, never to be seen at school again. While some children in her class did celebrate Christmas (some wrote about this as they explored family traditions and created a class quilt—see Figure 6.3), there are just some popular culture activities that are better kept at home if schools are to be places that sustain the cultures of children. This is but one example of we missteped and how we failed. Yet, we continue to learn from and with one another and from our personal and professional networks. We continue to strive for the truth that is already there.

THE CHILDREN COME FULL

In the opening words of the book, Haydée Dohrn Melendez-Morgan reminds us that "children come full, they come as full humans, full people, full." Writing about the world we need in order to see children as full humans, Paris (2021) enjoins:

> The current moment, full of so much pain and loss, but also brimming with hope and possibility for a more loving and just future, has invited us to better understand what we must divest from and invest in to more completely embrace such needed reclamation, transformation. I do not know where we will be in the pandemic when this article lands in your hands, but I do know our painful memories and losses, our ongoing movements toward justice and liberation, our learning about the world we need and deserve from this unrelenting time will be lasting, generational (p. 373).

Similarly, as this book closes, we invite you to consider the ways you might move through this painful moment in our current history and toward truths that are already there, toward a future of culturally sustaining pedagogies that will be lasting. We hope you are able to interpret and contextualize our models and stories and practices in your own context as you work toward a future where culturally sustaining early literacy pedagogies can uncover the truths that are already there. We hope this text can accompany you as you move toward a future of early language and literacy pedagogies that see, honor, and extend children in their fullness.

APPENDIX A

Children's Literature for Creating and Sustaining Communities

¡Sí! Somos Latinos by Alma Flor Ada and F. Isabel Campoy
Tablado de Dona Rosita by Alma Flor Ada and E. Isabel Campoy
I Love Saturdays y Domingos by Alma Flor Ada
How to Read a Book by Kwame Alexander
Njinga of Ndongo and Matamba by Ekiuwa Aire
Mi Musica: Somos Latinos by George Ancona, Alma Flor Ada, and F. Isabel Campoy
I Am Every Good Thing by Derrick Barnes
Crown: Ode to the Fresh Cut by Derrick Barnes
Ada Twist, Scientist by Andrea Beaty
Your Name Is a Song by Jamilah Thompson-Bigelow
My First Trip to Africa by 8-year-old Atlantis Tye Browder
Maya's Blanket/La Manta de Maya by Monica Brown
My Name Is Celia/Me Llamo Celia: The Life of Celia Cruz by Monica Brown
Tito Puente, Mambo King/Tito Puente: Rey del Mambo by Monica Brown
Side By Side/Lado a Lado by Monica Brown
I Am Enough by Grace Byers
Maybe Something Beautiful by F. Isabel Campoy
I Lost My Tooth in Africa by Penda Diakité
What a Wonderful Word: A Collection of Untranslatables from Around the World by Nicola Edwards and Luisa Uribe
We Rise, We Resist, We Raise Our Voices by Wade Hudson and Cheryl Willis Hudson
Salam Alaiakum: A Message of Peace by Harris J
Black Is a Rainbow Color by Angela Joy
The Colors of Us by Karen Katz
Carmella Full of Wishes by Matt de la Peña
Love by Matt de la Peña
Islandborn by Junot Díaz
Abuela by Arthur Dorros
I Choose series by Elizabeth Estrada
Stolen Words by Melanie Florence

131

Hip Hop Speaks to Children by Nikki Giovanni
When a Bully Is President: Truth and Creativity for Oppressive Times by Maya Christina Gonzalez
The Hill We Climb by Amanda Gorman
Amazing Faces by Lee Bennett Hopkins
I Walk with Vanessa: A Picture Book Story About a Simple Act of Kindness by Kerasoët
I Am René, the Boy/Soy René, el Niño by René Colato Laínez
René Has Two Last Names/René Tiene Dos Apellidos by René Colato Laínez
The Tooth Fairy Meets El Ratón Pérez by René Colato Laínez
Waiting for Papá/Esperando a Papá by René Colato Laínez
When the Beat Was Born: DJ Kool Herc and the Creation of Hip Hop by Laban Carrick Hill
I, Too, Am America by Langston Hughes
Please, Baby, Please by Spike Lee
Soccer Star by Mina Javaherbin
This Book Is Anti-racist: 20 Lessons on How to Wake Up, Take Action, and Do the Work by Tiffany Jewell
Sofia Martinez: Abuela's Birthday by Jaqueline Jules
On Monday When It Rained by Cheryl Kachenmeister
Big Red Lollipop by Rukhsana Khan
We Are the Water Protectors by Carole Lindstrom and Michaela Goade
Our Skin: A First Conversation about Race by Megan Maddison, Jessica Ralli, and Isabel Roxas
Juneteenth: A Children's Story by Opal Lee
Juneteenth: A Celebration by Courtney Juste
Alma and How She Got Her Name by Juana Martinez-Neal
One of a Kind, Like Me/Único Como Yo by Laurin Mayeno
Saturday by Oge Mora
Thank you, Omu! by Oge Mora
Dreamers by Yuyi Morales
We All Sing with the Same Voice by J. Phillip Miller and Sheppard M. Greene
I Know My Bill of Rights by Mysonne Linen and Heddrick McBride
Oh the Things That We're For by Innosanto Nogaro
You Are Mighty: A Guide to Changing the World by Caroline Paul
The Kissing Hand by Audrey Penn
Indigenous Peoples' Day by Katrina M. Phillips
The Sandwich Swap by Queen Rania Al Abdullah of Jordan and Kelly DiPucchio
My Brother Charlie by Holly Robinson Peete and Ryan Elizabeth Peete
¡El Fútbol es un Golazo! by Reading A-Z
The Word Collector by Peter H. Reynolds
If Dominican Were a Color by Sili Recio

My Name Is Yoon by Helen Recorvitz
When Jo Louis Won the Title by Belinda Rochelle
This Is Our House by Michael Rosen
Math Tricks by Kathy Schulz
My Many Colored Days by Dr. Seuss
Always Anjali by Sheetal Sheth
¡Solo Pregunta!/Just Ask by Sonia Sotomayor
We Are Still Here!: Native American Truths Everyone Should Know by Traci Sorrell
Charlotte and the Quiet Place by Deborah Sosin
Dear Primo: A Letter to My Cousin by Duncan Tonatiuh
Separate Is Never Equal: Sylvia Mendez and Her Family's Fight for Desegregation by Duncan Tonatiuh
Sometimes I'm Bombaloo by Rachel Vail
Owl Babies by Martin Wadell
I Lost My Tooth! by Mo Willems
Esquivel! Space-Age Sound Artist by Susan Wood
Each Kindness by Jaqueline Woodson
The Day You Begin by Jacqueline Woodson
Encounter by Jane Yolen
Malala's Magic Pencil by Malala Yousafzai

References

Adair, J. K. (2014). Agency and expanding capabilities in early grade classrooms: What it could mean for young children. *Harvard Educational Review, 84*(2), 217–241. https://doi.org/10.17763/haer.84.2.y46vh546h41l2144

Adair, J. K., Colegrove, K. S. S., & McManus, M. E. (2017). How the word gap argument negatively impacts young children of Latinx immigrants' conceptualizations of learning. *Harvard Educational Review, 87*(3), 309–334. DOI: 10.17763/1943-5045-87.3.309

Adesope, O. O., Lavin, T., Thompson, T., & Ungerleider, C. (2010). A systematic review and meta-analysis of the cognitive correlates of bilingualism. *Review of Educational Research, 80*(2), 207–245. https://doi.org/10.3102/0034654310368803

Afflerbach, P. (2017). *Understanding and using reading assessment, K-12*. ASCD.

Afflerbach, P., Pearson, P. D., & Paris, S. G. (2008). Clarifying differences between reading skills and reading strategies. *The Reading Teacher, 61*(5), 364–373. https://doi.org/10.1598/RT.61.5.1

Alim, S., & Paris, D. (2015). Whose Language Gap? Critical and Culturally Sustaining Pedagogies as Necessary Challenges to Racializing Hegemony. *Journal of Linguistic Anthropology, 25*(1), 79–80. https://doi.org/10.1111/jola.12071

Alim, S., & Paris, D. (2017). What is culturally sustaining pedagogy and why does it matter? In D. Paris & H. S. Alim (Eds.), *Culturally sustaining pedagogies: Teaching and learning for justice in a changing world* (pp. 1–24). Teachers College Press. https://doi.org/10.22329/JTL.V11I1.4987

Allington, R. L., McCuiston, K., & Billen, M. (2015). What research says about text complexity and learning to read. *The Reading Teacher, 68*(7), 491–501. DOI: 10.1002/trtr.1280

Alvarez, L. (2012). Reconsidering academic language in practice: The demands of Spanish expository reading and students' bilingual resources. *Bilingual Research Journal, 35*(1), 32–52. https://doi.org/10.1080/15235882.2012.667373

Anderson, R. C., Hiebert, E. H., Scott, J. A., & Wilkinson, I. A. G. (1985). *Becoming a nation of readers: The report of the commission on reading*. https://eric.ed.gov/?id=ED253865

Annamma, S. A. (2018). *The pedagogy of pathologization: Dis/abled girls of color in the school-prison nexus*. Routledge. DOI: 10.4324/9781315523057

Anyon, J. (1980). Social class and the hidden curriculum of work. *Journal of Education, 162*(1), 67–92. DOI: 10.1177/002205748016200106

Atkinson, R. C., & Shiffrin, R. M. (1968). Human memory: A proposed system and its control processes. In K. W. Spence & J. T. Spence (Eds.), *The*

References

psychology of learning and motivation: Advances in research and theory (pp. 89–195). Academic Press.

Au, K. H. (1979). Using the experience-text relationship method with minority children. *The Reading Teacher, 31*(1), 46–49.

Baines, J., Tisdale, C., & Long, S. (2018). *"We've been doing it your way long enough": Choosing the culturally relevant classroom.* Teachers College Press.

Baker, L., Afflerbach, P., & Reinking, D. (Eds.). (2012). *Developing engaged readers in school and home communities.* Routledge.

Baker-Bell, A. (2020). *Linguistic justice: Black language, literacy, identity, and pedagogy.* Routledge. https://doi.org/10.1080/09500782.2021.1972119

Bakhtin, M. M. (1984). *Esthétique de la création verbale/Speech genres and other essays.* Gallimard.

Baldwin, J. (1993). *Nobody knows my name: More notes of a native son.* Vintage.

Bartolomé, L. (1994). Beyond the methods fetish: Toward a humanizing pedagogy. *Harvard Educational Review, 64*(2), 173–195. DOI: 10.17763/haer.64.2.58q5m5744t325730

Bear, D. R., Invernizzi, M., Templeton, S., & Johnston, F. (2012). *Words their way with English learners: Word study for phonics, vocabulary and spelling.* Pearson.

Beck, I. L., McKeown, M. G., & Kucan, L. (2013). *Bringing words to life: Robust vocabulary instruction.* Guilford Press.

Beneke, M. R. (2019). Mapping the silence: The curriculum of dis/ability and race in preservice teachers' educational trajectories. *AERA Online Paper Repository.*

Beneke, M. R., Machado, E., & Taitingfong, J. (2022). Dismantling Carceral Logics in the Urban Early Literacy Classroom: Towards Liberatory Literacy Pedagogies with/for Multiply-Marginalized Young Children. *Urban Education,* Published online first, 00420859221091235. https://doi.org/10.1177/00420859221091235

Bentley, D. F., & Souto-Manning, M. (2019). *Pre-K stories: Playing with authorship and integrating curriculum in early childhood.* Teachers College Press.

Berliner, D. (2011). Rational responses to high stakes testing: The case of curriculum narrowing and the harm that follows. *Cambridge journal of education, 41*(3), 287–302. https://doi.org/10.1080/0305764X.2011.607151

Bialystok, E. (2011). Coordination of executive functions in monolingual and bilingual children. *Journal of Experimental Child Psychology, 110*(3), 461–468. DOI: 10.1016/j.jecp.2011.05.005

Biemiller, A., & Boote, C. (2006). An effective method for building meaning vocabulary in primary grades. *Journal of Educational Psychology, 98*(1), 44. DOI: 10.1037/0022-0663.98.1.44

Bishop, R. S. (1990). Mirrors, Windows, and Sliding Glass Doors. *Perspectives: Choosing and Using Books for the Classroom, 6*(3), ix–xi.

Bonilla-Silva, E. (2017). What we were, what we are, and what we should be: The racial problem of American sociology. *Social Problems, 64*(2), 179–187. https://doi.org/10.1093/socpro/spx006

Boutte, G. S. (2002). *Resounding voices: School experiences of people from diverse ethnic backgrounds.* Allyn & Bacon.

Boutte, G. S. (2015). *Educating African American students: And how are the children?* Routledge.

Boutte, G. S., & Johnson Jr., G. L. (2013). Funga Alafia: Toward welcoming, understanding, and respecting African American speakers' bilingualism and biliteracy.

Equity & Excellence in Education, 46(3), 300–314. https://doi.org/10.1080/10665684.2013.806850

Boutte, G. S., & Muller, M. (2018). Engaging children in conversations about oppression using children's literature. *Talking Points, 30*(1), 2–9. https://library.ncte.org/journals/TP/issues/v30-1/29853

Briceño, A., & Klein, A. F. (2019). A second lens on formative reading assessment with multilingual students. *The Reading Teacher, 72*(5), 611–621. DOI: 10.1002/trtr.1774

Camangian, P. R., & Cariaga, S. (2021). Social and emotional learning is hegemonic miseducation: Students deserve humanization instead. *Race Ethnicity and Education*, 1–21. https://doi.org/10.1080/13613324.2020.1798374

Carbo, M. (1987). Reading Styles Research. *Phi Delta Kappan, 68*(6), 431–435.

Chall, J. S. (1983). Literacy: Trends and explanations. *Educational Researcher, 12*(9), 3–8.

Chandler, M. C., Gerde, H. K., Bowles, R. P., McRoy, K. Z., Pontifex, M. B., & Bingham, G. E. (2021). Self-regulation moderates the relationship between fine motor skills and writing in early childhood. *Early Childhood Research Quarterly, 57*, 239–250. DOI: 10.1016/j.ecresq.2021.06.010

Chomsky, N. (1957). Logical Structure in Language. *Journal of the American Society for Information Science, 8*(4), 284.

Clay, M. (2013). *An observation survey of early literacy achievement*. Heinemann.

Clay, M. M. (1982). *Observing young readers: Selected papers*. Heinemann.

Clay, M. M. (1991). *Becoming literate: The construction of inner control*. Pearson.

Clay, M. M. (2001). *Change over time in children's literacy development*. Heinemann.

Clay, M. M. (2010). *How very young children explore writing*. Heinemann.

Cleaveland, L. B. (2016). *More about the authors: Authors and illustrators mentor our youngest writers*. Heinemann.

Coburn, C. E., Pearson, P. D., & Woulfin, S. (2011). Reading policy in the era of accountability. In M. Kamil, P. D. Pearson, E. Moje, & P. Afflerbach (Eds.), *Handbook of Reading Research, Volume IV* (pp. 587–619). Routledge.

Cooke, T. (1994). *Full, full, full of love*. Walker Books.

Cooper, A. J. (1988). *A Voice from the South*. Oxford, UK: Oxford University Press.

Cooperative Children's Book Center. (2019). Data on books by and about Black, Indigenous and People of Color published for children and teens. https://ccbc.education.wisc.edu/literature-resources/ccbc-diversity-statistics/books-by-about-poc-fnn/

del Carmen Salazar, M. (2013). A humanizing pedagogy: Reinventing the principles and practice of education as a journey toward liberation. *Review of Research in Education, 37*(1), 121–148. https://doi.org/10.3102/0091732X12464032

Delpit, L. (2006). *Other people's children: Cultural conflict in the classroom*. The New Press.

Delpit, L. (2012). *"Multiplication is for White people:" Raising expectations for other people's children*. The New Press.

DeVries, R., & Zan, B. (2012). *Moral classrooms, moral children: creating a constructivist atmosphere in early education*. Teachers College Press.

Domínguez, M. (2017). "Se hace puentes al andar": Decolonial teacher education as a needed bridge to culturally sustaining and revitalizing pedagogies. In D. Paris & H. S. Alim (Eds.), *Culturally sustaining pedagogies: Teaching and learning for justice in a changing world* (pp. 225–246). Teachers College Press.

Doucet, F. (2017). What does a culturally sustaining learning climate look like? *Theory into Practice*, *56*(3), 195–204. https://doi.org/10.1080/00405841.2017.1354618

Doucet, F., & Adair, J. (2018). Introduction: A vision for transforming early childhood research and practice for young children of immigrants and their families. *Bank Street Occasional Papers*, (39), 2.

Duke, N. K. (2020). When young readers get stuck. *Educational Leadership*, *78*(3), 26–33.

Duke, N. K., & Cartwright, K. B. (2021). The science of reading progresses: Communicating advances beyond the simple view of reading. *Reading Research Quarterly*, *56*, S25–S44. https://doi.org/10.1002/rrq.411

Duke, N. K., & Martin, N. M. (2011). 10 things every literacy educator should know about research. *The Reading Teacher*, *65*(1), 9–22. https://doi.org/10.1598/RT.65.1.2

Dumas, M. J. (2014). 'Losing an arm': Schooling as a site of black suffering. *Race Ethnicity and Education*, *17*(1), 1–29. https://doi.org/10.1080/13613324.2013.850412

Dunn, A. H. (2021). *Teaching on days after: Educating for equity in the wake of injustice*. Teachers College Press.

Dutro, E. (2010). What 'hard times' means: Mandated curricula, class-privileged assumptions, and the lives of poor children. *Research in the Teaching of English*, *44*(3), 255–291.

Dyson, A. H. (2013). *Rewriting the basics: Literacy learning in children's cultures*. Teachers College Press.

Dyson, A. H. (2015). The search for inclusion: Deficit discourse and the erasure of childhoods. *Language Arts*, *92*(3), 199.

Eagle-Shield, A., Paris, D., Paris, R., & San Pedro, T. (Eds.). (2020). *Education in movement spaces: Standing rock to Chicago freedom square*. Routledge.

Edwards, P. (2016). *New ways to engage parents: Strategies and tools for teachers and leaders, K–12*. Teachers College Press.

Ehri, L. C. (1991). Development of the ability to read words. In R. Barr, M. L. Kamil, P. B. Mosenthal, & P. D. Pearson (Eds.), *Handbook of reading research*, (Vol. 2, pp. 383–417). Lawrence Erlbaum Associates, Inc.

Ehri, L. C., Nunes, S. R., Willows, D. M., Schuster, B. V., Yaghoub-Zadeh, Z., & Shanahan, T. (2001). Phonemic awareness instruction helps children learn to read: Evidence from the National Reading Panel's meta-analysis. *Reading Research Quarterly*, *36*(3), 250–287. https://doi.org/10.1598/RRQ.36.3.2

Elson, K. (2019). How should we sing happy birthday? Reconsidering classroom birthday celebrations. *Rethinking Schools*, *33*(3), 52–57.

Elson, K., & Nash, K. T. (2020). Taking a Journey to The Land of All: Using Children's Literature to Explore Gender Identity with First Graders. *Bank Street Occasional Papers*, (44)4. Retrieved from https://educate.bankstreet.edu/occasional-paper-series/vol2020/iss44/4/

Embassy of Haiti. (2021). Celebration of Haiti's 212th Year of Independence. https://www.haiti.org/celebration-of-haiti-s-212th-year-of-independence/

Emdin, C. (2013). Pursuing the pedagogical potential of the pillars of hip-hop through urban science education. *The International Journal of Critical Pedagogy*, *4*(3). http://libjournal.uncg.edu/ijcp/article/view/352

Ertmer, P. A., & Newby, T. J. (2013). Behaviorism, cognitivism, constructivism: Comparing critical features from an instructional design perspective. *Performance Improvement Quarterly, 26*(2), 43–71. DOI: 10.1111/j.1937-8327.1993.tb00605.x

Fishman, J. A. (1967). Bilingualism with and without diglossia; diglossia with and without bilingualism. *Journal of Social Issues, 23*(2), 29–38. https://doi.org/10.1111/j.1540-4560.1967.tb00573.x

Fountas, I. C., & Pinnell, G. S. (2012). Guided reading: The romance and the reality. *The Reading Teacher, 66*(4), 268–284. https://doi.org/10.1002/TRTR.01123

Fountas, I. C., & Pinnell, G. S. (2016). *Fountas & Pinnell Benchmark Assessment System (1 and 2)*. Heinemann.

Fountas, I. C., & Pinnell, G. S. (2017). *Guided reading: Responsive teaching across the grades*. Heinemann.

Frankel, K. K., Becker, B. L. C., Rowe, M. W., & Pearson, P. D. (2016). From "What is Reading?" to What is Literacy? *Journal of Education, 196*(3), 7–17. https://doi.org/10.1177/002205741619600303

Freebody, P., & Luke, A. (1990). Literacies programs: Debates and demands in cultural context. *Prospect: An Australian Journal of TESOL, 5*(3), 7–16.

Friere, P. (1972). *Pedagogy of the oppressed*. Penguin Books.

Frith, U. (1985). Beneath the surface of developmental dyslexia. In K. E. Patterson, J. C. Marshall, & M. Coltheart (Eds.), *Surface dyslexia*. Erlbaum.

Fry, E. (1980). The new instant word list. *The Reading Teacher, 34*(3), 284–289.

García, O. (2009). Education, multilingualism and translanguaging in the 21st century. In T. Skutnabb-Kangas, R. Phillipson, A. K. Mohanty, & M. Panda (Eds.), *Social justice through multilingual education* (pp. 140–158). Multilingual Matters.

Gardner, H., & Hatch, T. (1989). Educational implications of the theory of multiple intelligences. *Educational Researcher, 18*(8), 4–10. https://doi.org/10.3102/0013189X018008004

Gay, G. (2017). *Culturally responsive teaching: Theory, research, and practice*. Teachers College Press.

Gee, J. P. (1999). Critical issues: Reading and the new literacy studies: Reframing the national academy of sciences report on reading. *Journal of Literacy Research, 31*(3), 355–374. DOI: 10.1080/10862969909548052

Gee, J. P. (2007). *Social linguistics and literacies: Ideology in discourses*. Routledge.

Genishi, C., & Dyson, A. H. (2009). *Children, language, and literacy: Diverse learners in diverse times*. New York, NY: Teachers College Press.

Gillanders, C. (2018). ¿Cómo Lo Escribo en Inglés o en Español? Writing in dual-language learners. *The Reading Teacher, 71*(4), 421–430.

Glossop, R. J. (1988). Language policy and a just world order. *Alternatives, 13*(3), 395–409.

Glover, M. (2009). *Engaging young writers, preschool-grade 1*. Heinemann.

González, N., Moll, L., & Amanti, C. (Eds.). (2005). *Fund of knowledge: Theorizing practices in households and classrooms*. Erlbaum.

Gonzalez, N., Moll, L. C., Floyd-Tenery, M., Rivera, A., Rendon, P., Gonzales, R., & Amanti, C. (1993). Teacher research on funds of knowledge: Learning from households. NCRCDSLL Educational Practice Reports. https://escholarship.org/uc/item/5tm6x7cm

Goodman, Y., Watson, D., & Burke, C. (1987). *Reading miscue inventory: Alternative procedures*. Richard C. Owen Publishers.

Gort, M., & Pontier, R. W. (2013). Exploring bilingual pedagogies in dual language preschool classrooms. *Language and Education, 27*(3), 223–245. https://doi.org/10.1080/09500782.2012.697468

Gort, M., & Sembiante, S. F. (2015). Navigating hybridized language learning spaces through translanguaging pedagogy: Dual language preschool teachers' languaging practices in support of emergent bilingual children's performance of academic discourse. *International Multilingual Research Journal, 9*(1), 7–25. DOI: 10.1080/19313152.2014.981775

Gough, P. B., Juel, C., & Griffith, P. L. (1992). Reading, spelling, and the orthographic cipher. In P. B. Gough, L. C. Ehri, & R. Treiman (Eds.), *Reading acquisition* (pp. 35–48). Lawrence Erlbaum Associates.

Gough, P. B., & Tunmer, W. E. (1986). Decoding, reading and reading disability. *Remedial and Special Education, 7*, 6–10. https://doi.org/10.1177/074193258600700104

Graham, S., Harris, K. R., Mason, L., Fink-Chorzempa, B., Moran, S., & Saddler, B. (2008). How do primary grade teachers teach handwriting? A national survey. *Reading and Writing, 21*(1), 49–69. https://doi.org/10.1007/s11145-007-9064-z

Grande, S., & McCarty, T. L. (2018). Indigenous elsewheres: Refusal and remembering in education research, policy, and praxis. *International Journal of Qualitative Studies in Education, 31*(3), 165–167.

Graves, D. H. (1983). *Writing: Teachers and children at work*. Heinemann.

Graves, M. F. (2016). *The vocabulary book: Learning and instruction*. Teachers College Press.

Gregory, E., Long, S., & Volk, D. (2004). *Many pathways to literacy: Young children learning with siblings, grandparents, peers and communities*. Routledge.

Guthrie, J. T. (2015). Growth of motivations for cognitive processes of reading. In P. D. Pearson & E. H. Hiebert (Eds.), *Research-based practices for teaching Common Core literacy*, (pp. 107–122). Teachers College Press.

Guthrie, J. T., & Klauda, S. L. (2014). Effects of classroom practices on reading comprehension, engagement, and motivations for adolescents. *Reading Research Quarterly, 49*(4), 387–416. https://doi.org/10.1002/rrq.81

Gutiérrez, K. D., & Johnson, P. (2017). Understanding identity sampling and cultural repertoires: Advancing learning in justice pedagogies. In D. Paris & H. S. Alim (Eds.), *Culturally sustaining pedagogies: Teaching and learning for justice in a changing world* (pp. 247–260). Teachers College Press.

Gutiérrez, K. D., & Rogoff, B. (2003). Cultural ways of learning: Individual traits or repertoires of practice. *Educational Researcher, 32*(5), 19–25. https://doi.org/10.3102/0013189X032005019

Hall, G., & Cook, G. (2012). Own-language use in language teaching and learning. *Language Teaching, 45*(3), 271–308. https://doi.org/10.1017/S0261444812000067

Halliday, M. A. K. (1978). *Language as Social Semiotic: The Social Interpretation of Language and Meaning*. Edward Arnold.

Harlin, R., & Souto-Manning, M. (2009). Review of research: Educating Latino children: International perspectives and values in early education. *Childhood Education, 85*(3), 182–186.

Hart, B., & Risley, T. R. (1995). *Meaningful differences in the everyday experience of young American children*. Paul H Brookes Publishing.

Harvey, S., & Goudvis, A. (2007). *Strategies that work: Teaching comprehension for understanding and engagement*. Stenhouse Publishers.

Heath, S. B. (1982). What no bedtime story means: Narrative skills at home and school. *Language in Society, 11*(1), 49–76. https://doi.org/10.1017/S0047404500009039

Helman, L. A., & Bear, D. R. (2007). Does an established model of orthographic development hold true for English learners. In *56th yearbook of the National Reading Conference* (pp. 266–280). National Reading Conference.

Hertz, C., & Mraz, K. (2018). *Kids 1st from Day 1: A Teacher's Guide to Today's Classroom*. Heinemann.

Hiebert, E. H. (2014). The forgotten reading proficiency: Stamina in silent reading. *Stamina, silent reading, and the common core state standards. Santa Cruz, CA: Text Project*.

Hill, M. L., & Petchauer, E. (Eds.). (2013). *Schooling hip-hop: Expanding hip-hop based education across the curriculum*. New York, NY: Teachers College Press.

Hoffman, J. V., Cabell, S. Q., Barrueco, S., Hollins, E. R., & Pearson, P. D. (2021). Critical issues in the science of reading: Striving for a wide-angle view in research. *Literacy Research: Theory, Method, and Practice*, 23813377211032195. DOI: 10.1177/23813377211032195

Hoffman, J. V., Martinez, R. A., & Danielson, K. (2016). Emerging reading and the social practice turn in literacy: Still becoming a nation of readers. *Journal of Education, 196*(3), 19–25. DOI: 10.1177/002205741619600304

Hollins, E. R. (2011). Teacher preparation for quality teaching. *Journal of Teacher Education, 62*(4), 395–407. https://doi.org/10.1177/0022487111409415

Hollins, E. R. (2015a). *Culture in school learning: Revealing the deep meaning* (3rd ed.). Routledge.

Hollins, E. R. (2015b). *Rethinking field experiences in preservice teacher preparation: Meeting new challenges for accountability*. Routledge.

Hollins, E. R. (2017). Literacy Learning and Teacher Preparation for Urban Students. *Kappa Delta Pi Record, 53*(4), 179–183. https://doi.org/10.1080/00228958.2017.1369281

Hollins, E. R. (2019). *Teaching to transform urban schools and communities: The power of pedagogy*. Routledge.

Hopkins, L. B., & Soentpiet, C. (2015). *Amazing faces*. Lee & Low Books.

Horn, M., & Giacobbe, M. E. (2007). *Talking, drawing, writing: Lessons for our youngest writers*. Stenhouse Publishers.

International Literacy Association. (2019). *Children experiencing reading difficulties: What we know and what we can do* (retrieved from literacy leadership brief: children experiencing reading difficulties). Newark, DE.

International Literacy Association. (2020). *Phonological awareness in early childhood literacy development* (position statement and research brief). Newark, DE.

Jones, C. D., & Reutzel, D. R. (2012). Enhanced alphabet knowledge instruction: Exploring a change of frequency, focus, and distributed cycles of review. *Reading Psychology, 33*(5), 448–464. https://doi.org/10.1080/02702711.2010.545260

Kelkar, A. S., Hough, M. S., & Fang, X. (2013). Do we think alike? A cross-cultural study of executive functioning. *Culture and Brain, 1*(2), 118–137. https://doi.org/10.1007/s40167-013-0010-4

Kinloch, V. (2010). "To not be a traitor of Black English": Youth perceptions of language rights in an urban context. *Teachers College Record, 112*(1), 103–141. DOI: 10.1177/016146811011200101

Kinloch, V. (2011). Innovative writing instruction: When it happens "across": Writing as transformative and expansive. *The English Journal, 100*(5), 95–99.

Kinloch, V. (2017). You ain't making me write. In D. Paris & H. S. Alim (Eds.), *Culturally sustaining pedagogies: Teaching and learning for justice in a changing world* (pp. 25–43). Teachers College Press.

Kinloch, V., Burkhard, T., & Penn, C. (2017). When school is not enough: Understanding the lives and literacies of black youth. *Research in the Teaching of English, 52*, 34–58.

Kirkland, D. E., & Hull, G. A. (2011). Literacy out of school: A review of research on programs and practices. In *Handbook of reading research* (Vol. IV, pp. 737–751).

Koplow, L. (2002). *Creating schools that heal: Real-life solutions*. Teachers College Press.

Koplow, L. (2021). *Emotionally responsive practice: A path for schools that heal, infancy-grade 6*. Teachers College Press.

Kriete, R., & Davis, C. (2014). *The morning meeting book*. Center for Responsive Schools, Inc.

Kuchirko, Y. (2019). On differences and deficits: A critique of the theoretical and methodological underpinnings of the word gap. *Journal of Early Childhood Literacy, 19*(4), 533–562. DOI: 10.1177/1468798417747029

LaBerge, D., & Samuels, S. J. (1974). Toward a theory of automatic information processing in reading. *Cognitive Psychology, 6*(2), 293–323. https://doi.org/10.1016/0010-0285(74)90015-2

Ladson-Billings, G. (1995). But that's just good teaching! The case for culturally relevant pedagogy. *Theory into Practice, 34*(3), 159–165. DOI: 10.1080/00405849509543675

Ladson-Billings, G. (2009). *The dreamkeepers: Successful teachers of African American children*. John Wiley and Sons.

Ladson-Billings, G. (2014). Culturally relevant pedagogy 2.0: Aka the remix. *Harvard Educational Review, 84*(1), 74–84. https://doi.org/10.17763/haer.84.1.p2rj131485484751

Ladson-Billings, G. (2017). The (R)evolution Will not be Standardized: Teacher Education, Hip Hop Pedagogy, and Culturally Relevant Pedagogy 2.0. In D. Paris & H. S. Alim (Eds.), *Culturally sustaining pedagogies: Teaching and learning for justice in a changing world* (pp. 141–156). New York, NY: Teachers College Press.

Laing, S. P., & Kamhi, A. (2003). Alternative assessment of language and literacy in culturally and linguistically diverse populations. *Language, Speech, and Hearing Services in Schools, 34*(1), 44–55. https://doi.org/10.1044/0161-1461(2003/005)

Laman, T. T. (2013). *From ideas to words: writing strategies for English language learners*. Heinemann.

Laman, T. T., & Henderson, J. W. (2018). "Welcome to Room 131": Putting Culturally Sustaining Pedagogies to Practice in a Second-Grade Classroom. *Talking Points, 30*(1), 18–26.

Lankshear, C., & Knobel, M. (2004). *A handbook for teacher research*. McGraw-Hill Education.

Larson, J., & Marsh, J. (2015). *Making literacy real: Theories and practices for learning and teaching*. SAGE.

Lee, C. D. (2017). An Ecological Framework for Enacting Culturally Sustaining Pedagogy. In H. S. Alim & D. Paris (Eds.), *Culturally sustaining pedagogies; teaching and learning for justice in a changing world*. Teachers College Press.

Lee & Low Books. (2017). Classroom Library Questionnaire. https://www.leeandlow.com/educators/grade-level-resources/classroom-library-questionnaire

Lee, T., & McCarty, T. (2017). Upholding indigenous education sovereignty through critical culturally sustaining/revitalizing pedagogy. In D. Paris & H. S. Alim (Eds.), *Culturally sustaining pedagogies: Teaching and learning for justice in a changing world* (pp. 61–82). Teachers College Press.

Lippi-Green, R. (2011). *English with an accent: Language, ideology, and discrimination in the United States*. Routledge.

Lipson, M. Y., Chomsky-Higgins, P., & Kanfer, J. (2011). Diagnosis: The missing ingredient in RTI assessment. *The Reading Teacher, 65*(3), 204–208. DOI: 10.1002/TRTR.01031

Long, S. (2017, August 7). Name Stories (personal communication).

Long, S., Hutchinson, W., & Neiderhiser, J. (2011). *Supporting students in a time of core standards: English language arts, grades prek-2*. Urbana, IL: National Council of Teachers of English.

Long, S., Souto-Manning, M., & Vasquez, V. (Eds.). (2016). *Courageous leadership in early childhood education: Taking a stand for social justice*. Teachers College Press.

Long, S., Volk, D., Baines, J., & Tisdale, C. (2013). 'We've been doing it your way long enough': Syncretism as a critical process. *Journal of Early Childhood Literacy, 13*(3), 418–439. https://doi.org/10.1177/1468798412466403

Lonigan, C. J., & Shanahan, T. (2009). Developing early literacy: Report of the National Early Literacy Panel. Executive summary. A Scientific synthesis of early literacy development and implications for intervention. National Institute for Literacy.

Love, B. L. (2019). *We want to do more than survive: Abolitionist teaching and the pursuit of educational freedom*. Beacon Press.

Luke, A., & Freebody, P. (1999). A map of possible practices: further notes on the four resources model. *Practically Primary, 4*(2), 5–8. https://search.informit.org/doi/10.3316/aeipt.96162

Lyiscott, J. (2014). *3 ways to speak English*. Ted Talk. https://www.ted.com/talks/jamila_lyiscott_3_ways_to_speak_english?language=en

Machado, E. (2017). Fostering and sustaining diverse literacy practices in the early childhood classroom: Reviewing the literature in three areas. *Literacy Research: Theory, Method, and Practice, 66*(1), 309–324. DOI: 10.1177/2381336917718178

Maldarelli, J. E., Kahrs, B. A., Hunt, S. C., & Lockman, J. J. (2015). Development of early handwriting: Visual-motor control during letter copying. *Developmental Psychology, 51*(7), 879. https://doi.org/10.1037/a0039424

Manyak, P. C., Manyak, A. M., & Kappus, E. M. (2021). Lessons from a Decade of Research on Multifaceted Vocabulary Instruction 75(1), 27–39. DOI: 10.1002/trtr2010

Martin-Jones, M., Blackledge, A., & Creese, A. (Eds.). (2012). *The Routledge handbook of multilingualism*. Routledge.

References

Martin Luther King Jr. Research and Education Institute. (1986, January 20). *King National Holiday*. https://kinginstitute.stanford.edu/

McCarthy, J. (2020). *Layers of learning: Using read-alouds to connect literacy and caring conversations*. Stenhouse Publishers.

McGeown, S. P., Osborne, C., Warhurst, A., Norgate, R., & Duncan, L. G. (2016). Understanding children's reading activities: Reading motivation, skill and child characteristics as predictors. *Journal of Research in Reading, 39*(1), 109–125. https://doi.org/10.1111/1467-9817.12060

McKenna, M. C., & Dougherty-Stahl, K. A. (2015). *Assessment for Reading Instruction* (3rd Edition). Guilford Press.

Miles, K. P., & Ehri, L. C. (2019). Orthographic mapping facilitates sight word memory and vocabulary learning. In D. Kilpatrick, R. Joshi, & R. Wagner (Eds.), *Reading Development and Difficulties* (pp. 63–82). Springer. DOI: 10.1007/978-3-030-26550-2_4

Miller, E. T. (2015). Discourses of whiteness and blackness: An ethnographic study of three young children learning to be white. *Ethnography and Education, 10*(2), 137–153. https://doi.org/10.1080/17457823.2014.960437

Miller, P. J., & Sperry, D. E. (2012). Déjà vu: The continuing misrecognition of low-income children's verbal abilities. In S. Fiske & H. R. Markus (Eds.), *Facing social class: How societal rank influences interaction* (pp. 109–130). Russell Sage Foundation.

Morrison, T. (1998, March). From an interview on *Charlie Rose*. Public Broadcasting Service. Retrieved from https://www.youtube.com/watch?v=-Kgq3F8wbYA

Morrow, L. M., Gambrell, L. B., Neuman, S. B., & Dickinson, D. K. (2002). *Literature-based instruction in the early years*. Guilford Press.

Muhammad, G. (2020). *Cultivating genius: An equity framework for culturally and historically responsive literacy*. Scholastic.

Nash, K. T. (2016). Out of the mouths of scholars. In P. Gorski, R. Salcedo, & L. Landsman (Eds.), *Talking back and looking forward: An educational revolution in poetry and prose*. Rowman and Littlefield.

Nash, K. T., Arce-Boardman, A., Luna, C., Panther, L., Thomas, R. K., & McNeil, H. (2021). My teaching comes from them: Mediating guided reading in a multilingual classroom. In S. Catapano & C. Thompson (Eds). The classroom library: A catalyst for change. Rowman and Littlefield.

Nash, K. T., Glover, C., & Polson, B. (Eds). (2020). *Toward culturally sustaining teaching: Early childhood educators honor children with practices for equity and change*. Routledge.

Nash, K. T., & Panther, L. (2019). The children come full: From high leverage to humanizing and culturally sustaining literacy practices in urban schools. *Teachers College Record, 121*(4). https://www.tcrecord.org/Content.asp?ContentId=22669

Nash, K. T., Panther, L., & Arce-Boardman, A. (2018). La historia de mi nombre: A culturally sustaining early literacy practice. *The Reading Teacher, 71*(5), 605–60. DOI: 10.1002/trtr.1665

Nash, K., Panther, L., & Elson, K. (2019). Student-created book basket labels: An innovative, culturally sustaining literacy practice. *The Reading Teacher, 72*(6), 755–760. DOI: 10.1002/trtr.1782

Nash, K. T., & Piña, P. (2020). Translanguaging as culturally sustaining literacy teaching in a dual-language preschool classroom. In K. T. Nash, C. Glover, &

B. Polson (Eds.), *Honoring children: New approaches, strategies, and practices for culturally sustaining early literacy teaching*. Routledge.

Nash, O. M. (2021). Inventing inherited moral deficit: Racial pathologism in historical perspective. https://history.throughourowneyes.com/racial-pathologism-in-historical-context

National Reading Panel. (2000). *Report of the national reading panel: Teaching children to read: An evidence-based assessment of the scientific research literature on reading and its implications for reading instruction*. National Institute of Child Health and Human Development, National Institutes of Health.

National Writing Project. (2022). *Teaching Writing*. Retrieved from https://archive.nwp.org/cs/public/print/resource_topic/teaching_writing.

Noddings, N. (2012). The caring relation in teaching. *Oxford Review of Education, 38*(6), 771–781.

Noguera, P. A., & Alicea, J. A. (2020). Structural racism and the urban geography of education. *Phi Delta Kappan, 102*(3), 51–56. https://doi.org/10.1177/0031721720970703

Noguerón-Liu, S. (2020). Expanding the knowledge base in literacy instruction and assessment: Biliteracy and translanguaging perspectives from families, communities, and classrooms. *Reading Research Quarterly, 55*, S307–S318. DOI: 10.1002/rrq.354

Osorio, S. L. (2020). Building culturally and linguistically sustaining spaces for emergent bilinguals: Using read-alouds to promote translanguaging. *The Reading Teacher, 74*(2), 127–135. https://doi.org/10.1002/trtr.1919

Ouellette, G. P. (2006). What's meaning got to do with it: The role of vocabulary in word reading and reading comprehension. *Journal of Educational Psychology, 98*(3), 554. DOI: 10.1037/0022-0663.98.3.554

Owocki, G., & Goodman, Y. (2002). *Kidwatching: Documenting children's literacy development*. Heinemann.

Pacheco, M. B., & Miller, M. E. (2016). Making meaning through translanguaging in the literacy classroom. *The Reading Teacher, 69*(5), 533–537. https://doi.org/10.1002/trtr.1390

Paris, D. (2009). "They're in my culture, they speak the same way": African American language in multiethnic high schools. *Harvard Educational Review, 79*(3), 428–448. https://doi.org/10.17763/haer.79.3.64j4678647mj7g35

Paris, D. (2012). Culturally sustaining pedagogy: A needed change in stance, terminology, and practice. *Educational Researcher, 41*(3), 93–97. https://doi.org/10.3102/0013189X12441244

Paris, D. (2016). "It was a black city": African American language in California's changing urban schools and communities. In S. Alim, J. Rickford, & A. Ball, (Eds.), *Raciolinguistics: How language shapes our ideas about race*. Oxford University Press. DOI:10.1093/acprof:oso/9780190625696.003.0014

Paris, D. (2019). Naming beyond the white settler colonial gaze in educational research. *International Journal of Qualitative Studies in Education, 32*(3), 217–224. https://doi.org/10.1080/09518398.2019.1576943

Paris, D. (2021). Culturally sustaining pedagogies and our futures. *The Educational Forum* 85(4), 364–376. https://doi.org/10.1080/00131725.2021.1957634

Paris, D., & Alim, H. S. (2014). What are we seeking to sustain through culturally sustaining pedagogy? A loving critique forward. *Harvard Educational Review, 84*(1), 85–100. https://doi.org/10.17763/haer.84.1.982l873k2ht16m77

Paris, D., & Alim, H. S. (2017a). *Culturally sustaining pedagogies: Teaching and learning for justice in a changing world.* Teachers College Press.
Paris, D., & Alim, S. (2017b) in Ferlazzo, L. (2017, July 6). Author interview: Culturally sustaining pedagogies. *EdWeek.* Retrieved from http://blogs.edweek.org/teachers/classroom_qa_with_larry_ferlazzo/2017/07/author_interview_culturally_sustaining_pedagogies.html?qs=django+paris
Paris, D., & Winn, M. T. (Eds.). (2013). *Humanizing research: Decolonizing qualitative inquiry with youth and communities.* Sage Publications.
Pearson, P. D. (2004). The reading wars. *Educational Policy, 18*(1), 216–252.
Pearson, P. D., & Hiebert, E. H. (Eds.). (2015). *Based practices for teaching common core literacy.* Teachers College Press.
Pearson, P. D., Hiebert, E. H., & Kamil, M. L. (2007). Vocabulary assessment: What we know and what we need to learn. *Reading Research Quarterly, 42*(2), 282–296. https://doi.org/10.1598/RRQ.42.2.4
Pinnell, G. S., & Fountas, I. C. (2010). *The continuum of literacy learning, grades K-8: Behaviors and understandings to notice, teach, and support.* Heinemann.
Pollock, M. (Ed.). (2008). *Everyday antiracism: Getting real about race in school.* The New Press.
Pollock, M. (2009). *Colormute.* Princeton University Press.
Puranik, C. S., & Lonigan, C. J. (2011). From scribbles to scrabble: Preschool children's developing knowledge of written language. *Reading and Writing, 24*(5), 567–589. DOI: 10.1007/s11145-009-9220-8
Purcell-Gates, V., Melzi, G., Najafi, B., & Orellana, M. F. (2011). Building literacy instruction from children's sociocultural worlds. *Child Development Perspectives, 5*(1), 22–27.
Quinn, M. F., & Bingham, G. E. (2019). The nature and measurement of children's early composing. *Reading Research Quarterly, 54*(2), 213–235. https://doi.org/10.1002/rrq.232
Ray, K. W. (2010). *In pictures and in words.* Heinemann.
Ray, K. W., & Cleaveland, L. (2004). *About the authors.* Heinemann.
Ray, K. W., & Cleaveland, L. (2016). *More about the authors.* Heinemann.
Ray, K. W., & Glover, M. (2008). *Already ready: nurturing writers in preschool and kindergarten.* Heinemann.
Rodgers, E., D'Agostino, J. V., Berenbon, R., Johnson, T., & Winkler, C. (2021). Scoring Running Records: Complexities and affordances. *Journal of Early Childhood Literacy,* 14687984211027198. doi:10.1177/14687984211027198
Rogoff, B. (2003). *The cultural nature of human development.* Oxford University Press.
Rosa, J. (2019). *Looking like a language, sounding like a race.* Oxford University Press.
Rosa, J., & Flores, N. (2017a). Unsettling race and language: Toward a raciolinguistic perspective. *Language in Society, 46*(5), 621–647. DOI: 10.1017/S0047404517000562
Rosa, J., & Flores, N. (2017b). Do you hear what I hear? Raciolinguistic ideologies and culturally sustaining pedagogies. In D. Paris & H. S. Alim (Eds.), *Culturally sustaining pedagogies: Teaching and learning for justice in a changing world* (pp. 175–190). Teachers College Press.
Rosenblatt, L. M. (1994). *The reader, the text, the poem: The transactional theory of the literary work.* SIU Press.

San Pedro, T., & Kinloch, V. (2017). Toward projects in humanization: Research on co-creating and sustaining dialogic relationships. *American Educational Research Journal, 54*(1), 373S–394S. https://doi.org/10.3102/0002831216671210

Sanders M. G., & Epstein J. L. (2005). School-family-community partnerships and educational change: International perspectives. In A. Hargreaves (Ed.), *Extending educational change*. Springer, Dordrecht. https://doi.org/10.1007/1-4020-4453-4_10

Schott Foundation for Public Education. (n.d.). Restorative practices: A guide for educators. Schott Foundation. http://schottfoundation.org/restorative-practices

Schwartz, G. L., & Jahn, J. L. (2020). Mapping fatal police violence across US metropolitan areas: Overall rates and racial/ethnic inequities, 2013–2017. *PloS One, 15*(6), e0229686. https://doi.org/10.1371/journal.pone.0229686

Seravallo, J. (2017). *The writing strategies book*. Heinemann.

Seymour, P. H., Aro, M., Erskine, J. M., & Collaboration with COST Action A8 Network. (2003). Foundational literacy acquisition in European orthographies. *British Journal of Psychology, 94*(2), 143–174.

Shanahan, T. (2020a). What constitutes a science of reading instruction?. *Reading Research Quarterly, 55*(2), 235–247. https://doi.org/10.1002/rrq.349

Shanahan, T. (2020b). Limiting children to books they can already read: Why it reduces their opportunity to learn. *American Educator, 44*(2), 13. https://www.aft.org/ae/summer2020/shanahan

Share, D. L. (2008). On the Anglocentricities of current reading research and practice: The perils of overreliance on an "outlier" orthography. *Psychological Bulletin, 134*(4), 584. DOI: 10.1037/0033-2909.134.4.584

Silverman, R. D., Proctor, C. P., Harring, J. R., Hartranft, A. M., Doyle, B., & Zelinke, S. B. (2015). Language skills and reading comprehension in English monolingual and Spanish–English bilingual children in grades 2–5. *Reading and Writing, 28*(9), 1381–1405. DOI: 10.1007/s11145-015-9575-y

Smagorinsky, P. (2001). If meaning is constructed, what is it made from? Toward a cultural theory of reading. *Review of Educational Research, 71*(1), 133–169. https://doi.org/10.3102/00346543071001133

Smith, D. (2018). Telling our stories, sharing our lives. In L. Johnson, G. S. Boutte, & D. Smith (Eds.), *African diaspora literacy: The heart of transformation in K–12 schools and teacher education*, (pp. 107–128). Rowman and Littlefield.

Smitherman, G. (2006). *Word from the mother: Language and African Americans*. Routledge.

Smolkin, L. B., & Donovan, C. A. (2000). *The contexts of comprehension: Information book read alouds and comprehension acquisition*. Center for the Improvement of Early Reading Achievement.

Souto-Manning, M., & Yoon, H. S. (2018). *Rethinking early literacies: Reading and rewriting worlds*. Routledge.

Spencer, T. G., Falchi, L., & Ghiso, M. P. (2011). Linguistically diverse children and educators (re) forming early literacy policy. *Early Childhood Education Journal, 39*(2), 115–123.

Stahl, K. A. D., Flanigan, K., & McKenna, M. C. (2019). *Assessment for reading instruction*. Guilford Publications.

Stahl, S. A., & Yaden, Jr., D. B. (2004). The development of literacy in preschool and primary grades: Work by the center for the improvement of early reading achievement. *The Elementary School Journal, 105*, 141–165. DOI: 10.1086/428862

Stenner, A. J. (1996, February). *Measuring reading comprehension with the Lexile framework*. Fourth North American Conference on Adolescent/Adult Literacy, Washington, D.C. https://eric.ed.gov/?id=ED435977

Stone, K. (2017). *Reconsidering primary literacy: Enabling children to become critically literate*. Routledge.

Street, B. V. (1995). *Social literacies: Critical approaches to literary development*. Longman.

Street, B. V., & Street, B. B. (1984). *Literacy in theory and practice* (Vol. 9). Cambridge University Press.

Sulzby, E., & Teale, W. (1991). Emergent literacy. In R. Barr, M. L. Kamil, P. B. Mosenthal, & P. D. Pearson (Eds.), *Handbook of reading research: Volume II* (pp. 727–757). Longman.

Taberski, S. (2017). *Comprehension from the ground up: Simplified, sensible instruction for the K-3 reading workshop*. Heinemann.

Tamis-LeMonda, C. S., Kuchirko, Y., Luo, R., Escobar, K., & Bornstein, M. H. (2017). Power in methods: Language to infants in structured and naturalistic contexts. *Developmental science*, 20(6), e12456. DOI: 10.1111/desc.12456

Teachers College Reading and Writing Project. (2020). Resources for Teaching and Learning. https://readingandwritingproject.org/resources

Teachers College Reading and Writing Project Concepts of Print Assessment. (2020). https://readingandwritingproject.org/resources/foundational-skills-assessments

Templeton, S. (2020). Stages, Phases, Repertoires, and Waves: Learning to Spell and Read Words. The Reading Teacher (74), 3, 315–323. https://doi:10.1002/trtr.1951

Thomas, E. E. (2016). Stories still matter: Rethinking the role of diverse children's literature today. *Language Arts*, 94(2), 112.

Tolentino, E. P. (2007). "Why do you like this page so much?" Exploring the potential of talk during preschool reading activities. *Language Arts*, 84(6), 519–528.

Tuck, E. (2009). Suspending damage: A letter to communities. *Harvard Educational Review*, 79(3), 409–428. https://doi.org/10.17763/haer.79.3.n0016675661t3n15

Valdés, G., Fishman, J. A., Chávez, R., & Pérez, W. (2008). Maintaining Spanish in the United States: Steps toward the effective practice of heritage language reacquisition/development. *Hispania*, 91(1), 4–24.

van Bergen, E., Vasalampi, K., & Torppa, M. (2021). How are practice and performance related? Development of reading from age 5 to 15. *Reading Research Quarterly*, 56(3), 415–434. https://doi.org/10.1002/rrq.309

Vasquez, V. M. (2014). *Negotiating critical literacies with young children*. Routledge.

Vygotsky, L. S. (1978). *Mind in society: The development of higher psychological processes*. Harvard University Press.

Vygotsky, L. S. (1997). *The collected works of LS Vygotsky: Problems of the theory and history of psychology* (Vol. 3). Springer Science and Business Media.

Wasik, B. A., Hindman, A. H., & Snell, E. K. (2016). Book reading and vocabulary development: A systematic review. *Early Childhood Research Quarterly*, 37, 39–57. https://doi.org/10.1016/j.ecresq.2016.04.003

Wasik, B. A., & Iannone-Campbell, C. (2012). Developing vocabulary through purposeful, strategic conversations. *The Reading Teacher*, 66(4), 321–332. https://doi.org/10.1002/TRTR.01095

Wheeler, R., Cartwright, K. B., & Swords, R. (2012). Factoring AAVE into reading assessment and instruction. *The Reading Teacher*, 65(6), 416–425. https://doi.org/10.1002/TRTR.01063

Willis, A. I. (2015). Literacy and race: Access, equity, and freedom. *Literacy Research: Theory, Method, and Practice, 64*(1), 23–55. https://doi.org/10.1177/2381336915617617

Wise, C. (2022, February). A culturally responsive vocabulary intervention. Talk given at the University of Maryland Baltimore County.

Wohlwend, K. E. (2013). Play, literacy, and the converging cultures of childhood. In J. Larson & J. Marsh (Eds.), *The Sage Handbook of Early Childhood Literacy* (2nd ed., pp. 80–95). London: Sage.

Woodson, C. G. (1933). *The mis-education of the Negro*. Book Tree.

Wynter-Hoyte, K., Braden, E. G., Rodriguez, S., & Thornton, N. (2019). Disrupting the status quo: Exploring culturally relevant and sustaining pedagogies for young diverse learners. *Race, Ethnicity, and Education, 22*(3), 428–447. https://doi.org/10.1080/13613324.2017.1382465

Yama, H., & Zakaria, N. (2019). Explanations for cultural differences in thinking: Easterners' dialectical thinking and Westerners' linear thinking. *Journal of Cognitive Psychology, 31*(4), 487–506. https://doi.org/10.1080/20445911.2019.1626862

Yatvin, J. (2002). Babes in the woods: The wanderings of the National Reading Panel. *Phi Delta Kappan, 83*(5), 364–369.

Yoon, H. S. (2015). Assessing children in kindergarten: The narrowing of language, culture and identity in the testing era. *Journal of Early Childhood Literacy, 15*(3), 364–393. https://doi.org/10.1177/1468798414548778

Zapata, A., & Laman, T. T. (2016). "I write to show how beautiful my languages are": Translingual writing instruction in English-dominant classrooms. *Language Arts, 93*(5), 366–378.

Zentella, A. C. (2015). Books as the magic bullet. *Journal of Linguistic Anthropology, 25*(1), 75–77. https://doi.org/10.1111/jola.12071

Index

Accountability-based assessments, 112
Affixes spelling, 95
African American Language (AAL), 45, 56–57
Agreements, community, 24–27
Al Abdullah, Jordan, 30
Alexander, Kwame, 51
Alim, S., 6, 126
Alphabet and word walls, 46–47
Amazing Faces (Hopkins), 46
Ancestral knowledge, 58
Areas, seating, 21–23
Assessments, 112
   accountability-based, 112
   defined, 113
   everyday, 114–115
   high-stakes, 112–113
   purpose of, 113–114
   seven overarching principles, 113–114
Assignment, seats, 22–23
Authentic vocabulary assessments, 121–122
Authors, mentor, 51

Barnes, Derrick, 34, 55–56
Bartolomé, L., 61
Beneke, M. R., 7
Black Lives Matter, 34–35
Book-basket labels, 39–40
Books
   displaying, 21
   making, 50–51
   selection of, 19–21
Bottom-up processing, 48
Boutte, G.S., 7, 63
Braden, E. G., 7
Burke, C., 54

Byers, Grace, 30, 71

Carceral logics, 14
Cartwright, K. B., 55
Celebrations, 32
Centering languages, 68–69
Chants, 76–77
Charlotte and the Quiet Place (Sosin), 51
Checklists, 115
Child-created book-basket labels, 39–40
Children literature, 131–133
Choice time, spaces for, 23–24
Cipher, 31, 35
Classroom community, 13
   as spaces, 14
Classroom jobs, 29
Classroom library, 19–21, 22, 61–70
   culturally sustaining, resources for building, 62
   knowingness through, 39
Classroom schedule, 27, 28
Classroom setting, 18–24
   classroom library, 19–21
   meeting spaces, 18–19
   seating areas, 21–23
   spaces for choice time, 23–24
Clay, M. M., 54, 117
Cleaveland, L., 50
Cole, Robert, 30
Communal love, 14
Communication, family, 15
Community agreements and expectations, 24–27
Complex reading models, 54–55
Comprehension, 60
Concepts of Print (CAP), 116

Conferences, 114
Conferring, 99–100
Confianza, 15, 25
Conflicts, resolving, 30–32
Context-based reading models, 54–55
Counterpractices, 7
Critical questions, 62–63
Critical socioculturalism, 5
Crown: An Ode to the Fresh Cut (Barnes), 55–56
Cultural knowledge, 55–56
Culturally mediated cognition, 58–59
Culturally sustaining early literacy teaching, 8
  interpretive framework, 9
Culturally sustaining literacy teaching practices
  defined, 3
Culturally sustaining pedagogies (CSPs), 4, 6–8, 13, 53–54
  defined, 6
  features of, 6–7
  interpretive framework for early childhood, 10
Culturally sustaining reading practices, 61
Culturally sustaining writing instruction, 97–109
Culture, 3
Culture of poverty, 45

Decodable texts, 68
Decoding, 60
Delpit, L., 59
Derivational relations spelling, 95
Dictation, 109
DiPucchio, Kelly, 30
Dominant English (DE), 45
Doucet, F., 7, 14
Duke, N. K., 55
Dyson, A. H., 50, 69–70, 113

Each Kindness (Woodson), 30
Early letter-name alphabetic spelling, 95
Editing, revising and, 100–101
English
  complexity of, 45–46
Everyday assessments, 114–115
Everyday talk, 62–63

Executive function, 58
Expectations, community agreements and, 24–27
Expressive vocabulary, 80

Family communication, 15
Fluency, 60
Fluid stages
  of spelling, 95–96
  of writing, 92–94
Freebody, P., 55
Fry, E., 47

Games, play and, 77–79
Gatherings
  informal playground, 15–16
  of stories, 16–17
Genishi, C., 50, 69–70, 113
Genres, 104–105
Glover, M., 50
Gonzalez, Maya Christina, 63
Goodman, Y., 54
Greenbelt writing, 104
Group writing, 106
Guided reading, 66
  small groups for, 66–67
Gutiérrez, K. D., 45

Handwriting, 90–91, 106–108
Hearing and Recording Sounds in Words, 123–124
Henderson, J. W., 7
High-frequency words, 47, 108–109, 121
High-stakes assessment, 112–113
Hollins, E. R., 9, 48
Home visits, 17–18
Hopkins, Lee Bennett, 46
How to Read a Book (Alexander), 51
Humanism, 5
Humanizing, culturally sustaining reading model, 55–61
  culturally mediated cognition, 58–59
  motivation to read, 59
  ways of being, 57
  ways of knowing, 55–57
  ways of reading, 57–58
Hybridized spaces, 48
Hybridized writing workshop, 97–106

Index

I Am Enough (Byers), 30, 42, 71
I Am Every Good Thing (Barnes & James), 34
Identity texts
    knowingness through creating, 40–43
Illustrators, 51
Independent reading, 65
Independent writing, 98–99
Informal playground gatherings, 15–16
Interactive read-aloud, 69–70, 75, 81–83
Interactive writing, 106

James, Gordon, 34
Jewell, Tiffany, 63
Jobs, classroom, 29
Justice, kindness as, 30–31

Kindness, as justice, 30–31
Kinloch, V., 24
The Kissing Hand (Penn), 21
Knowingness, 35
    through classroom library, 39
    through creating identity texts, 40–43
    fostering through morning meetings, 35–37
    through letter, sound, and word work, 45–48
    through naming, 37–38
Knowledge
    ancestral, 58
    cultural, 55–56
    procedural, 24
Koplow, L., 16

Ladson-Billings, G., 6
Laman, T. T., 7
Language
    centering, 68–69
    children abilities, 72
    oral, 72–80
Late letter-name alphabetic spelling, 95
Learning teaching as an interpretive process (LTIP), 9
Learning theories, 5–6
    North Star, 4–5
Lee, Spike, 21
Lee, Tonya Lewis, 21
Letter, knowingness through, 45–48

Letter and sound naming, 116–117
Letter-identification assessment, 117
Library, classroom. *See* Classroom library
Life-affirming ways of reading, 61
Line of regression, 8
Literacy
    defined, 3
Literacy assessment. *See* Assessment
Literature, children, 131–133
Love, B. L., 3
Luke, A., 55
Lyiscott, J., 45

Machado, E., 7
Math Tricks (Schulz), 86
Meaning sorts, 86
Medina, Jane, 46
Meetings
    morning, 35–37, 73–74
    spaces, 18–19
Mentor authors, 51
Middle letter-name alphabetic spelling, 95
Mini-lesson, 97, 98
The Morning Meeting Book (Kriete & Davis), 35
Morning meetings, 73–74
    fostering knowingness through, 35–37
Motivation for reading, 59
Muhammad, G., 4, 111
Muller, M., 7, 63
Multifaceted vocabulary instruction, 80–81
Multilingual children, 123
Musical bookends, 76
Musical joyfulness, 76–77

Naming, knowingness through, 37–38
North Star learning theories, 4–5
Notebook, thinking, 49–50
Note-taking, 114

Oppression, reading and writing against, 63–64
Oral language, 72–73
    development, 73–80
    multimodal tools, 79–80
Osorio, S. L., 7
Owl Babies (Wadell), 21

Paris, D., 6, 126
Pattern sorts, 84
Penn, Audrey, 21
Phonemic awareness, 46, 122–124
Phonological awareness, 46
Photos, 115
Planning notes, 114–115
Play, and games, 77–79
Please, Baby, Please (Lee & Lee), 21
Primary spelling inventory (PSI), 122
Procedural knowledge, 24

Quality vocabulary instruction, 81
Quantity instruction, 81
Questionnaire, 20, 62–63

Raciolinguistics, 56–57
Ray, K. W., 50
Reader's Theater, 86–87
Readiness, 112
Reading
  guided, 66
  high-frequency word, 121
  independent, 65
  models. *See* Reading models
  motivation for, 59
  against oppression, 63–64
  strategic processes of, 57
  strategies, 59–61
  ways of, 57–58
Reading aloud, 43–44
Reading models
  context-based/complex, 54–55
  humanizing, culturally sustaining, 55–61
  simple/rope/stage, 54
Reading workshop, 51–52
Receptive vocabulary, 80
Response to intervention (RTI), 113
Revising and editing, 100–101
Rodriguez, S., 7
Rogoff, B., 45
Rope reading models, 54
Routines
  classroom, 27–29
  writing workshop, 49–51
Running records, 118–121

The Sandwich Swap (Al Abdullah & DiPucchio), 30
Schedule, classroom, 27, 28
Schulz, Kathy, 86
Scripted phonics curricula, 47–48
Seating areas, 21–23
Sentence dictation, 109
Sentence stems, 74–75
Separate Is Never Equal: Sylvia Mendez and Her Family's Fight for Desegregation (Tonatiuh), 63, 90
Seravallo, J., 98
Share time, 37, 101
Simple reading models, 54
Singing, 77
Small groups, for guided reading, 66–67
Smith, D., 13, 18
Social constructivism, 6
Socioculturalism, 5
Sosin, Deborah, 51
Sound, knowingness through, 45–48
Sound sorts, 84
Spaces
  for choice time, 23–24
  hybridized, 48
  meeting, 18–19
Spelling, 122–124
  fluid stages of, 95–96
  inventories, 122–123
Stage reading models, 54
The Story of Ruby Bridges (Cole), 30
Strategies, reading, 59–61
Strategy instruction, 81
Superficial notion of community, 13
Syllables and affixes spelling, 95

Teachers
  book selection, 19–21
Texts
  complexity, 64
  decodable, 68
  identity, 40–43
  intentional selection of, 67–68
Thinking notebook, 49–50
Think–turn–talk, 76
This Book Is Anti-racist: 20 Lessons on How to Wake Up, Take Action, and Do the Work (Jewell), 63
Thornton, N., 7

Tonatiuh, Duncan, 63, 90
Top-down processing, 48
Toward Culturally Sustaining Teaching: Early Childhood Educators Honor Children with Practices for Equity and Change (Nash), 6

Units, writing, 102–104

Vasquez, V. M., 89
Vocabulary, 60, 121–122
  development, 80–87

Wadell, Martin, 21
Watson, D., 54
Ways of being, 57
Ways of knowing, 55–57
Ways of reading, 57–58
  life-affirming, 61
When a Bully Is President: Truth and Creativity for Oppressive Times (Gonzalez), 63
Within-word pattern spelling, 95
Woodson, Jacqueline, 30
Word identification, 60
Word sorts, 84–86
Word walls, 46–47, 83–84
Words, high-frequency, 47, 108–109, 121

Writerly selves, development of, 50, 94
Writing
  celebrations, 105–106
  culturally sustaining instruction, 97–109
  development, 90–92
  fluid stages of, 92–94
  genres, 104–105
  greenbelt, 104
  hybridized workshop, 97–106
  independent, 98–99
  interactive and group, 106
  against oppression, 63–64
  tools, 102
  units, 102–104
Writing process, 97
The Writing Strategies Book (Seravallo), 98
Writing workshop routines, 49–51
  developing writerly selves, 50
  making books, 50–51
  mentor authors and illustrators, 51
  thinking notebook, 49–50
Wynter-Hoyte, K., 7

Yoon, H. S., 117

Zentella, A. C., 58

About the Authors

Alicia Arce-Boardman is in her 14th year teaching as a bilingual and dual language education teacher. She currently teaches 2nd and 3rd grade in a loop. Alicia identifies as Latinx—her mother's family is from Paraguay and her father's is from Mexico. Alicia's explicit dedication to culturally relevant teaching began in 2013 when she was a dyad in the Professional Dyads and Culturally Relevant Teaching (PDCRT). Alicia strives to foreground children's voices as she works as a guide in the classroom community. When Alicia is not teaching children and college students, she enjoys being a dance mom and traveling with her husband and three children.

Kerry Elson is in her 11th year of teaching and has been teaching in New York public schools for 6 years. Kerry, who identifies as White and able-bodied, first learned about culturally relevant, critical sociocultural, and social constructivist teaching methods as a student at Bank Street College of Education and as an assistant teacher at Bank Street School for Children, the College's laboratory school. She currently teaches kindergarten and 1st grade in a loop. When Kerry isn't teaching, she likes spending time with friends, trying new restaurants, and writing short humor pieces about guinea pigs, theater, food, and more.

Haydée Dohrn-Melendez Morgan is in her 18th year of teaching, and has been teaching kindergarten, 1st grade, and pre-kindergarten in New York City public schools for 13 years. She teaches 3-year-old kindergarten and pre-kindergarten in a loop at a school in East Harlem. Haydée, who is Puerto Rican, also considers her life's work laughing with her husband and riding on their motorcycle, where she is often fueled by the beauty of nature, and learning and growing as a mother of two teenage children who inspire her to be present in all moments and to notice the magic in a smile.

Kindel Turner Nash is the Spangler Distinguished Professor of Early Childhood Literacy at Appalachian State University in Boone, North Carolina. Kindel is White and connected to the Black community by marriage. She was a public school teacher and literacy specialist (grades pre-K–8) in urban or urban-like contexts for 10 years prior to becoming a teacher educator. When Kindel isn't writing or teaching future teachers, she enjoys playing her Martin guitar with her Dad, long rambling walks, gardening, southern-style dinners, poetry, and discussing philosophy, religion, identity and history with her husband and children.

Roderick Peele is in his 8th year of teaching. Roderick has taught 1st-, 2nd-, 3rd-, and 5th-grade scholars in inclusion and general education settings. Currently, he teaches 2nd and 3rd grade in a loop. Roderick identifies as Black and a descendant of African ancestors who were enslaved in the southern United States. Roderick's encounters with culturally relevant teaching took place during his 2nd year of teaching when he searched for more books with Black and Latinx protagonists and stumbled across Dr. Gloria Ladson-Billings' work. Even though she coined the title, at age 13, Roderick had already been introduced to these ideas within *The Mis-Education of the Negro* by Dr. Carter G. Woodson (1933/2006). Roderick loves being surrounded by the thoughts, ideas, and questions of his scholars.